CREATION'

Embracing Light Journal

Deborah A. Goshorn-Stenger

Our mission is to share the love of Jesus through His Word, nature, and creativity. We believe that God's beauty is all around us, if we'll pause to see it, and give Him honor and praise.

2 Pause and Praise Creations

Creation's Kaleidoscope: Embracing Light Journal (Volume 1)

Copyright 2021 © by 2 Pause and Praise Creations

All rights reserved. No part of this publication may be reproduced, stored in a retrieval system, or transmitted, in any form or by any means—electronic, mechanical, photocopying, recording, or otherwise—without prior written permission.

Requests for information should be directed to:
2 Pause and Praise Creations
5315 Long Street, Suite 518
McFarland, WI 53558

ISBN: 978-1-954690-01-1

Amplified Bible (AMP) Copyright © 2015 by The Lockman Foundation, La Habra, CA 90631. All rights reserved.; Christian Standard Bible (CSB) The Christian Standard Bible. Copyright © 2017 by Holman Bible Publishers. Used by permission. Christian Standard Bible®, and CSB® are federally registered trademarks of Holman Bible Publishers, all rights reserved.; Contemporary English Version (CEV) Copyright © 1995 by American Bible Society; English Standard Version (ESV) The Holy Bible, English Standard Version. ESV® Text Edition: 2016. Copyright © 2001 by Crossway Bibles, a publishing ministry of Good News Publishers.

GOD'S WORD Translation (GW) Copyright © 1995, 2003, 2013, 2014, 2019, 2020 by God's Word to the Nations Mission Society. All rights reserved.; Good News Translation (GNT) Copyright © 1992 by American Bible Society; Holman Christian Standard Bible (HCSB) Copyright © 1999, 2000, 2002, 2003, 2009 by Holman Bible Publishers, Nashville Tennessee. All rights reserved.; International Children's Bible (ICB) The Holy Bible, International Children's Bible® Copyright© 1986, 1988, 1999, 2015 by Tommy Nelson™, a division of Thomas Nelson. Used by permission.

International Standard Version (ISV) Copyright © 1995-2014 by ISV Foundation. ALL RIGHTS RESERVED INTERNATIONALLY. Used by permission of Davidson Press, LLC.; King James Version (KJV) Public Domain; Lexham English Bible (LEB) 2012 by Logos Bible Software. Lexham is a registered trademark of Logos Bible Software; Living Bible (TLB) The Living Bible copyright © 1971 by Tyndale House Foundation. Used by permission of Tyndale House Publishers Inc., Carol Stream, Illinois 60188. All rights reserved.; The Message (MSG) Copyright © 1993, 2002, 2018 by Eugene H. Peterson.

New American Standard Bible (NASB) New American Standard Bible®, Copyright © 1960, 1971, 1977, 1995, 2020 by The Lockman Foundation. All rights reserved.; New International Version (NIV) Holy Bible, New International Version®, NIV® Copyright ©1973, 1978, 1984, 2011 by Biblica, Inc.® Used by permission. All rights reserved worldwide.; New King James Version (NKJV) Scripturetaken from the New King James Version®. Copyright © 1982 by Thomas Nelson. Used by permission. All rights reserved.

New Living Translation (NLT) Holy Bible, New Living Translation, copyright © 1996, 2004, 2015 by Tyndale House Foundation. Used by permission of Tyndale House Publishers, Inc., Carol Stream, Illinois 60188. All rights reserved.

Tree of Life Version (TLV) Tree of Life (TLV) Translation of the Bible. Copyright © 2015 by The Messianic Jewish Family Bible Society.; The Voice (VOICE) The Voice Bible Copyright © 2012 Thomas Nelson, Inc. The Voice™ translation © 2012 Ecclesia Bible Society All rights reserved.

With Dedication

Dear Jesus,
This is our offering of love, gratitude, and praise. May every line, be like a song unto Your throne.

Dear Douglas,
I offer you a heartfelt "thank you" for being my right-hand—to hold as we walk, daily—to pray with, work with, to live and love with, in every step of this project. You're my best friend, and my earthly and heavenly treasure! I love you, and cherish every day of our journey.

Dear Family and Friends, to those who "*believed*" in me, and the talent given by God's Spirit—to bring His creations to life—I appreciate your support, and notes of encouragement.

A very special thank you, to my early readers/reviewers. I treasure your kindness and insights for this endeavor!

In loving memory of my Mom, *Pauline Rubeck Goshorn*, I'm thankful because you were my cheerleader and sharer of poems (as you've dubbed them "spiritual blessings") for many years. May God reward you for your part in this ministry on earth, and for His kingdom. We love you and appreciate every life you've helped touch with God's love.

I am grateful to each of you, my readers and fellow-journalers, and pray that this Volume of *Creation's Kaleidoscope*, will bring you blessing, joy, and God's grace, nearly and dearly, to your hearts.

In His Love,

deborah goshorn-stenger

Also by Deborah Goshorn-Stenger

The *Creation's Kaleidoscope* Series:

<u>Available Now</u>
Embracing Light (Volume I)
Devotional	Paperback and Ebook
Journal	Paperback
To-Go	Paperback, Exclusively on our website

<u>Please check our website for release dates for Volumes II/III.</u>

Let Everything that has Life … Praise (Volume II)
Devotional	Paperback and Ebook
Journal	Paperback
To-Go	Paperback, Exclusively on our website

Prisms of God's Glory (Volume III)
Devotional	Paperback and Ebook
Journal	Paperback
To-Go	Paperback, Exclusively on our website

To Contact us: 2PauseandPraiseCreations.com
or by mail at:
2 Pause and Praise Creations
5315 Long St, Suite 518
McFarland, WI 53558

"The Lord bless you and keep you; the Lord make His face shine upon you, and be gracious to you; the Lord lift up His countenance upon you, and give you peace." Numbers 6:24-26 NKJV

Preface

Do you remember the wonder that you felt as a child, when you discovered, the kaleidoscope? At first, you may have thought, "What is this?" After all, from the outside it looks ordinary enough. Some of them are void of design, while others are printed or wrapped in bright colors and designs. Yet, it isn't until you pick up this tube and peer inside, that you discover a magical world, an intricate place of imagination, that this "toy" seems to come to life.

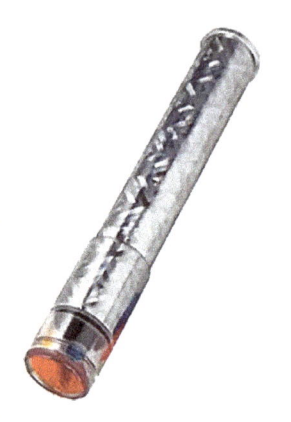

Well, one day I was pondering (you might say daydreaming), as part of my meditation with the Lord, when I began to wonder what God sees from heaven. In my mind, I began to form myriad kaleidoscopes. Just envision the earth's colors from subtle to vivid, from an arial view. Imagine every source of light from the heavenlies, touching earth. Imagine textures, colors and designs, and all living things that God has made, as they form facets, prisms, and fragmented designs. Then, pause to behold Him.

All of creation seemed to come alive, as if I was viewing it, for the first time. These, seemed to dance in the circle of my mind, as if forming a crown. And perhaps, that is exactly what all of creation is/does, before our Creator.

Then I began to think how our Creator's heart must have skipped a beat, as He formed every living thing in the Genesis account: light, the sun, moon, stars, came—out of nothing—into perfection, to display from the inside, out, the facets of God's love.

Next, I thought about creating a journal—how many of you have struggled with a blank page? Have you ever used this type, and thought "I don't know where to begin?" Have you never journaled at all? Or, are you an experienced "journaler" yet are searching for a creative, inspirational space that speaks to your heart?

With these things in mind, I set out to fashion—a meditative space to accompany *Creation's Kaleidoscope*—where you can pause and praise God. Here, you can take an action-step of faith, as you journey with Him, daily. So we've fashioned pages that invite you, to discover the Lord's beauty in creation.

There are pages to ponder His nature, places to ask and answer some questions, prayers (to inspire your own), and plenty of room for you to record your thoughts and to simply commune, grow, and rest in His grace. Periodically throughout the journal, you will find art pages, for you to express your creativity. Each, will have a suggested exercise to inspire you. These combine, to gently guide your time with God.

Like the kaleidoscope must be lifted, raised to a light source, and turned—getting to know the Lord requires us to draw close, to be still, and to seek to know Him. As we pick up His Word and peer into the wonders that He has made—He performs miracles. He transforms the fragmented things of our lives, into works of art.

Come, you're invited to explore God's Word, His majestic world, and some moments in His company. Come, pause, like the turning of a kaleidoscope's wand, to behold His intricate, imaginative, and interesting marvels. Come, discover the many facets of His character and loving-kindness.

It's my prayer that these photographs, poems, book excerpts, quotes, and journaling spaces— fill your imagination with inspiration—to pause and praise God, today, and every day of your life.

How to Use this Journal

This journal can be used alone, but is recommended to accompany the first book in this series. You will notice that it is themed to match its content. Prepare your heart with the ideas below, but step 1, is to come to meet God with a prayerful attitude.

The *Pause*:
- You're invited to read an entry or two from *Creation's Kaleidoscope: Embracing Light Devotional.* You'll notice the book and the journal (which contains a lot of new material) will highlight God's Word.
- Meditate upon the entry and the verse(s) provided. Think about what you have read. Absorb the truth, and ask God to speak the lesson into your mind for a personal application.
- Pause, to appreciate something of the imagery that has been presented on the page, or in God's majestic world.

The *Praise*:
- Thank Him for a few things in your life, and for what He has shown you, by taking this time in His company.
- Record a prayer or a few lines of worship unto our Creator, great God, and Abba Daddy.

If you will *Pause and Praise* as part of your journaling process, you will see and be documenting, a trail of God's faithfulness which will lead to greater trust, and growth in your spiritual life.

Prelude:

A Journaling Prayer

Dear Lord,
I come into this quiet space;
I come, bringing moments,
That are deliberately set aside,
To meet with You.

    I have been made in Your image;
    I am given value,
    By the amazing love,
    Which You show me, daily.

        I ask You, Jesus, to lead me,
        And guide me in Your ways.
        Speak into my heart,
        Into my mind.
        Block the voice of the enemy,
        And fill my thoughts with Your Word,
        Your promises,
        Your goodness, mercy and grace.

        Your Spirit is alive,
        Upon the earth,
        And in creation;
        Be alive, in me.

    I desire Your Will,
    And I surrender, Jesus,
    To Your perfect plan.
    Grant me peace,
    So that I rest in Your care.
    This day and all that happens in it,
    I submit to You.

I ask You to calm my thoughts,
And to focus my heart upon You,
And the meditations that I am about to receive.
Amen.

I encourage you to begin each meditation time with this prayer ...

So let's begin where it all began ... Genesis 1, 2:2 VOICE (Excerpts)

"In the beginning, God created everything: the heavens above and the earth below. Here's what happened: At first the earth lacked shape and was totally empty, and a dark fog draped over the deep while God's spirit-wind hovered over the surface of the empty waters. Then there was the voice of God.

God: Let there be light.

And light flashed into being. God saw that the light was beautiful and good, and He separated the light from the darkness. God named the light 'day' and the darkness 'night.' Evening gave way to morning. That was day one.

God: Let there be a vast expanse in the middle of the waters. Let the waters above part from the waters below.

So God parted the waters and formed this expanse, separating the waters above from the waters below. It happened just as God said. And God called the vast expanse 'sky.' Evening gave way to morning. That was day two.

God: Let the waters below the heavens be collected into one place and congregate into one vast sea, so that dry land may appear.

It happened just as God said. God called the dry land 'earth' and the waters congregated below 'seas.' And God saw that His new creation was beautiful and good.

God: Earth, sprout green vegetation! Grow all varieties of seed-bearing plants and all sorts of fruit-bearing trees.

It happened just as God said. The earth produced vegetation—seed-bearing plants of all varieties and fruit-bearing trees of all sorts. And God saw that His new creation was beautiful and good. Evening gave way to morning. That was day three.

God: Lights, come out! Shine in the vast expanse of heavens' sky dividing day from night to mark the seasons, days, and years. Lights, warm the earth with your light.

So God created huge sea creatures, all the swarm of life in the waters, and every kind and species of flying birds—each able to reproduce its own kind. And God saw that His new creation was beautiful and good. And God spoke this blessing over them. ...

… **God**: Be fruitful and multiply. Let creatures fill the seas. Let birds reproduce and cover the earth.

Evening gave way to morning. That was day five.

God: Earth, generate life! Produce a vast variety of living creatures—domesticated animals, small creeping creatures, and wild animals that roam the earth.

It happened just as God said. God made earth-creatures in a vast variety of species: wild animals, domesticated animals of all sizes, and small creeping creatures, each able to reproduce its own kind. God saw that His new creation was beautiful and good. And God paused.

God: Now let Us conceive a new creation—humanity—made in Our image, fashioned according to Our likeness. And let Us grant them authority over all the earth—the fish in the sea and the birds in the sky, the domesticated animals and the small creeping creatures on the earth.

So God did just that. He created humanity in His image, created them male and female. Then God blessed them and gave them this directive: 'Be fruitful and multiply. Populate the earth. I make you trustees of My estate, so care for My creation and rule over the fish of the sea, the birds of the sky, and every creature that roams a
the earth.'

God (to humanity): Look! I have given you every seed-bearing plant that grows on the earth and every fruit-bearing tree. They will be your food and nourishment. As for all the wild animals, the birds in the sky, and every small creeping creature—everything that breathes the breath of life—I have given them every green plant for food.

And it happened just as God said. Then God surveyed everything He had made, savoring its beauty and appreciating its goodness. Evening gave way to morning. That was day six. …

… On the seventh day—with the canvas of the cosmos completed—God paused from His labor and rested."

God created all things, by the sound of His voice. What is He saying to you, through creation, at this present time in your life? Have you been listening and observing His signs?

Setting the Scene: Out of Darkness

"At first the earth lacked shape and was totally empty, and a dark fog draped over the deep while God's spirit-wind hovered over the surface of the empty waters. Then there was the voice of God.

God*: Let there be light.*

And light flashed into being. God saw that the light was beautiful and good, and He separated the light from the darkness." Genesis 1:1-5 VOICE (Excerpts)

Likewise, the kaleidoscope's interior lies dormant—until it's lifted up to a source of light. Then, it reveals miracles of color, design, facets, and wonders to behold. From a veiled interior that gave you only a dim view, now radiate images that encourage your imagination to run free.

Did you ever think of dawn as a treasure, that dispels every shadow and illuminates all the amazing things that our Creator has made from the beginning of time? Have you ever seen light, as a form of God's embrace to all mankind?

Let the Lord shine His light into every corner of your mind, heart, and life.

Earth was Void

Out of void,
    Out of utter nothingness,
        Out of silence,
            Out of shapeless, fathomless darkness,
                God created heaven and earth.

Oddly enough, Ian's first word was "light."

★ Purple reminds me that Jesus is king.

What in creation, most inspires your mind?

What colors and images draw you to see God, in all of His loving facets?

~ The human brain ~
reds and yellows bring forth light, blues and greens are part of God's mystery. When I think of God, I see Him as a blue light (always constant, tried and true blue) at least, that is how it is to me. Blue tends to calm my fears, but at the same time, blue can make me anxious. Especially in a body of water where I can't see my feet.

"If I rise on the wings of the dawn, if I settle on the far side of the sea, even there your hand will guide me, your right hand will hold me fast." Psalm 139:9-10 NIV

God never changes — His power is infinite yet unpredictable.

God gave us two lights—the sun for day, the moon for night—so that we'd look up to behold Him and know His love is constant 24/7 and 365 days a year.

Did you ever think of dawn as a treasure, that dispels every shadow and illuminates all the amazing things that God has made from the beginning of time?

It was in the beginning, that God made all of the wonders that we see. He made galaxies and starry hosts, calling them each by name. He formed land and the seas, sea-life, all vegetation, flora and fauna, animals, livestock, birds, and insects—each in their own types and varieties. Then He breathed life, out of dust, to create mankind.

Which of these wonders most leaves you, in awe?

....

....

....

....

....

....

....

....

....

....

....

....

....

....

....

....

....

....

In six days, the Lord made all things, then He declared everything to be beautiful and "good." Then, He rested. Imagine it. All of heaven's majesty was in place. All of earth's miracles and delights were on display. Out of the void, came life, from the Creator, Life-Giver, Artist, Architect, Painter, Potter, and Sculptor, to show us the existence of nature and to demonstrate His own, so that no one is without excuse: to see Him, know Him, experience Him.

In the columns below, please write each title provided (i.e. Creator, Artist, Painter, etc.). After each, please jot a few adjectives to describe God's nature. Then rest, and let these absorb into your mind.

…………………………………….   …………………………………….

…………………………………….   …………………………………….

…………………………………….   …………………………………….

…………………………………….   …………………………………….

…………………………………….   …………………………………….

…………………………………….   …………………………………….

…………………………………….   …………………………………….

…………………………………….   …………………………………….

…………………………………….   …………………………………….

…………………………………….   …………………………………….

…………………………………….   …………………………………….

…………………………………….   …………………………………….

…………………………………….   …………………………………….

…………………………………….   …………………………………….

Even the Darkness ...

A beautiful sense of hush was lowering over the trees, and the first stars were on the rise in this location.

In another area of the world, dawn was beginning to break; light was beginning to shine forth.

What a solace to our minds when we feel troubled, lonely, or are hurting. Right?

Darkness, is not so, to our Father. He is awake at all hours, available in every circumstance, in any space of void, time of grief, difficulty, or when we find our hearts racing with anxiety. And to me, it brings comfort, that nothing can separate us from His love. No shadow. No sin. No lack on our part. Nothing that we do or don't do.

How does this truth, bring your mind rest and your soul a sense of peace?

....
....
....
....
....

Darkness—it's a physical state, meaning a lack of light. It can also mean an emotional state, as well—of illness, depression, sadness, or when circumstances weigh heavily on one's mind and spirit.

Are you feeling darkness—physically, emotionally, or spiritually? Below, express it to the Lord, and ask Him to bring you insights and deliverance.

....
....
....
....
....
....
....
....
....
....
....
....
....
....
....
....

Let the Lord shine His light into every corner of your mind, heart, and life. He's the One you can trust—always. He is the One Who is the Light of the World and heaven.

....

....

....

Father, when we feel darkness, void, or loneliness settle around our shoulders, or enter our minds and hearts, may Your light pierce every space, to disarm the shadows. For in You, is peace. In You, I find rest. In You, I am held from dusk to dawn, because I am loved by the One Who has written in the stars, His love for all mankind. Shine upon me Lord, right where I am, for I trust in You. Amen.

Here's space to write your own prayer.

....

....

....

....

....

....

....

....

....

....

....

....

....

....

"I have told you these things, so that in me you may have peace. In this world you will have trouble. But take heart! I have overcome the world."
John 16:33 (NIV)

Darkness and Light

Darkness and light, fight, compete—at every turn—in nature, in our emotions, in the spiritual realm (Ephesians 6:12). Yet darkness is not so, to the Lord. (Psalm 139:12) He rules above it, beneath it, over it, through it, in it. In fact, we enter into the world, enveloped in spiritual darkness, having a sinful nature from the moment of our birth. (Romans 3:23) Yet Jesus made a way for us to be pure—by being our sacrificial Lamb. (1 Peter 1:17-19) This is His invitation of love to us. It's His grace shining down into the heart as illumination in order to become our Lord and Savior.

Please look up the verses above, and record your insights.

Light shines as a flame, as a beacon. Yet, no matter its intensity—it breaks up shadows with a single touch; so too, our God!

"I sought the Lord, and He answered me and delivered me from all my fears. Those who look to Him are radiant with joy; their faces will never be ashamed." Psalm 34:4-5 HCSB

Darkness and light will always be at war, but peace is found in knowing Jesus. Since Jesus is the Light of the World, how can He shine through you in practical ways, to be a witness in times of trial, temptation, or when someone is attacking your beliefs or stand for Christ?

....

....

....

....

....

Darkness can be a covering for sin. Has God's light illuminated any area of your life with His truth? How about any area that needs to be changed? Any area that He wants greater trust and faith?

....

....

....

....

....

Soul's Introspection

Somehow fears, doubts and concerns seem to become magnified in the darkness.

Here, is where we need to take the fight to Satan. This is where we learn that Scripture memorization is our greatest weapon against his wily ways and that God fights for us.

What is your greatest area of struggle? What is your favorite Biblical promise, in defense?

....
....
....
....
....
....
....
....
....
....
....
....
....
....

> *"I call on you, my God, for you will answer me; turn your ear to me and hear my prayer. Show me the wonders of your great love, you who save by your right hand those who take refuge in you from their foes. Keep me as the apple of your eye; hide me in the shadow of your wings …" Psalm 17:6-8 (ESV)*

We may be lying on our side, on our back or stomach, but if we are calling upon the name of Jesus in the dark, light is in the midst of the room, and in our hearts. What's your heart's cry in the night?

....

....

....

....

....

....

....

....

> "I remembered my songs in the night. My heart meditated and my spirit asked: 'Will the Lord reject forever? Will he never show his favor again?' ... Then I thought, 'To this I will appeal: the years when the Most High stretched out his right hand. I will remember the deeds of the Lord; yes, I will remember your miracles of long ago. I will consider all your works and meditate on all your mighty deeds.'" Psalm 77:6-7, 10-12 NIV

....

....

....

....

....

....

....

....

....

....

....

You're beloved by Your Creator, Maker, and Abba Daddy.

How did an earthly parent, display love as the heavenly Father might? Or was this missing in your life? Give praise, if the first is true. And ask God to show you His perfect love, if the second applies.

"Fear not,
for I am with you;
be not dismayed,
for I am your God;
I will strengthen you,
I will help you,
I will uphold you
with my righteous
right hand."
Isaiah 41:10
(ESV)

Luxuriate like the Lizard

I found this lizard, luxuriating in the sun. He had just come from the undergrowth of bushes, to lounge on the bricks.

When was the last time that you simply came before the Lord, to rest, and do, likewise? Pause, make room. Sit, bow, kneel or lie prostrate on the floor … and let God speak … then record whatever "light" He reveals to your heart.

………………………………………………………………………………

………………………………………………………………………………

………………………………………………………………………………

………………………………………………………………………………

………………………………………………………………………………

………………………………………………………………………………

………………………………………………………………………………

………………………………………………………………………………

………………………………………………………………………………

………………………………………………………………………………

………………………………………………………………………………

………………………………………………………………………………

May the Light of Christ dwell in you, above you, beneath you, over you, through you—until your soul is illuminated—from within and from without. Because when He's Your Savior, Shepherd and Lord—darkness, has met its match. It's already been defeated on your behalf.

....

....

....

....

....

....

....

....

....

Peace comes in knowing the Light of the World. Thank God, below, for how He has brought a sense of solace to a place of darkness, to illuminate it with His love.

....

....

....

....

....

....

....

....

The Blank Page

A blank page is a fresh perspective. It's the gift of a new day to treasure. It's the opportunity to let go of something, in order to make room, for God to create something new.

In the space below, what does God want you to leave behind, so that He can do just that? Write or draw whatever comes to mind.

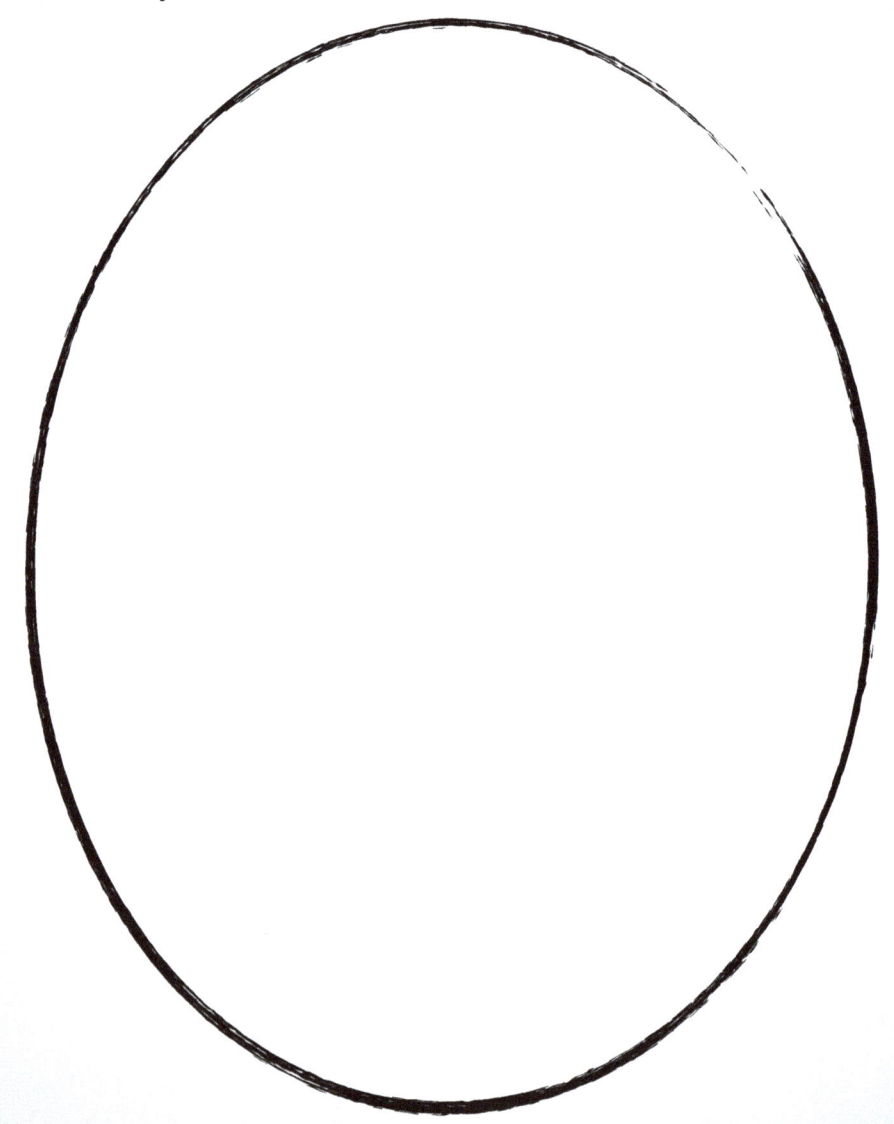

How did what you wrote or drew, show you that God was present?

"The Eternal is my light amidst my darkness and my rescue in times of trouble. So whom shall I fear? He surrounds me with a fortress of protection. So nothing should cause me alarm." Psalm 27:1 VOICE

Abba Daddy, I feel a void in the area of _____. But I am coming before You, as a child. I am laying it down at Your feet. Please remove this darkness. Shine Your light of love and hope into my heart, I pray. And bring healing to this space. For I want to trust You, with even, this. Show me how, Jesus. Amen.

....
....
....
....
....
....
....
....

> *All of creation is made by God, and points to His majesty, power, and grace.*

God speaks to us in many ways. But creation, more than any other method, seems to bring His attributes, to life. These are visible from the moment we wake in the morning, until we close our eyes in sleep at night. And if earth is His voice piece; heaven is His megaphone. But the wise, hear both within the soul, calling, to know Him as Lord.

Earth's Ballad

At the sound of Your voice ...
Darkness became light,
The sun, moon and stars,
Began to record our days.
    The birdsong began,
    Creating lyrics.
        The rivers and waves,
        Pour out a symphony,
        Of Your power, mercy and grace.
            The flowers, plants and gardens,
            Perform measure upon measure,
            Of Your glory and creativity.
The trees, fields, and mountains,
Display Your heart of love.
                All, combine as music,
                To invite us to know You,
                And to sing Your praise.

        Here's mine:

....

....

....

....

....

....

....

....

....

....

....

....

"I will praise the Lord at all times; His praise will always be on my lips." Psalm 34:1 HCSB

God sings over you with joy.

"You love him even though you have never seen him; though not seeing him, you trust him; and even now you are happy with the inexpressible joy that comes from heaven itself. And your further reward for trusting him will be the salvation of your souls." 1 Peter 1:8-9 TLB

Soul's Introspection

Praise can lift our hearts out of darkness, despair, depression. But we must choose to lift our eyes—off ourselves, our concerns, our circumstances—and onto His love, mercy and grace. If you're in a "pit," what are some first steps to reaching out for help? How can we prepare ahead of time, to defend ourselves, spiritually? And how can we encourage one another, when a friend or family member, goes through a period of loss or grief?

....

....

....

....

....

....

....

....

....

....

....

....

....

....

....

"May you be made strong with all the strength which comes from his glorious power, so that you may be able to endure everything with patience. And with joy give thanks to the Father, who has made you fit to have your share of what God has reserved for his people in the kingdom of light. He rescued us from the power of darkness and brought us safe into the kingdom of his dear Son, by whom we are set free, that is, our sins are forgiven." Colossians 1:12-15 GNT

Holy Hush

It is evening,
It is very early morning,
All is quiet, all is still;
Only creation sounds can be heard.
Calm descends.
Love transcends.
All else fades away.
There is only God and us,
And a holy hush,
Where His Spirit whispers, calls.
It communicates more than a shout or a proclamation.
In this stillness, our soul unfurls like dawn.
Awakening,
To shine.

"The people who sat in darkness have seen a great light, and upon those who sat in the region and shadow of death Light has dawned." Matthew 4:16 NKJV

You are known by name.

....
....
....
....
....
....
....

*God loved you so much—
that while He died for the world—
your face flashed before His eyes.*

....
....
....
....
....
....
....
....
....
....
....
....

God knows your voice.

"God called the light 'day,' and the darkness he called 'night.' And there was evening, and there was morning—the first day."
Genesis 1:5 NIV

To catch a glimpse of creation, is to hold a little child-like wonder in our hearts, no matter our age. Great is Your faithfulness, indeed, O God. Each morning, I will pause to behold You and give You my praise. Amen.

"Satisfy us in the morning with your steadfast love, that we may rejoice and be glad all our days."
Psalm 90:14 ESV

They say that it is darkest just before the dawn. This is true in terms of daylight, but it can also be applied to an emotional or spiritual circumstance. Have you experienced this personally? If so, what has "void" taught you? How did finding light, change your situation?

....

....

....

....

....

....

....

....

....

....

....

....

....

....

....

....

"For this reason we have not stopped praying for you since the day we heard about you. We ask God to fill you with the knowledge of his will through every kind of spiritual wisdom and insight. We ask this so that you will live the kind of lives that prove you belong to the Lord. Then you will want to please him in every way as you grow in producing every kind of good work by this knowledge about God." Colossians 1:9-10 GW

How has the Lord used a time in your life that felt like you were alone, to now show you, that He was present all along?

Dear Lord, creation is like a prayer from Your heart, to my soul. Every new sunrise, is a promise that You are with me. Every night, the moon and stars, are reminders of Your care—of Your presence throughout the night.

With each beautiful thing that You display, I, in turn, give You praise and prayer—my heart is lifted as an offering to Your soul. This is the dance of love between us. It is to be one with You, united as creation with Creator, and as Your child with my Abba Daddy. Amen.

....

....

....

....

....

....

....

....

....

....

....

....

....

....

"Honor and majesty surround Him; strength and beauty fill His sanctuary." Psalm 96:6 NLT

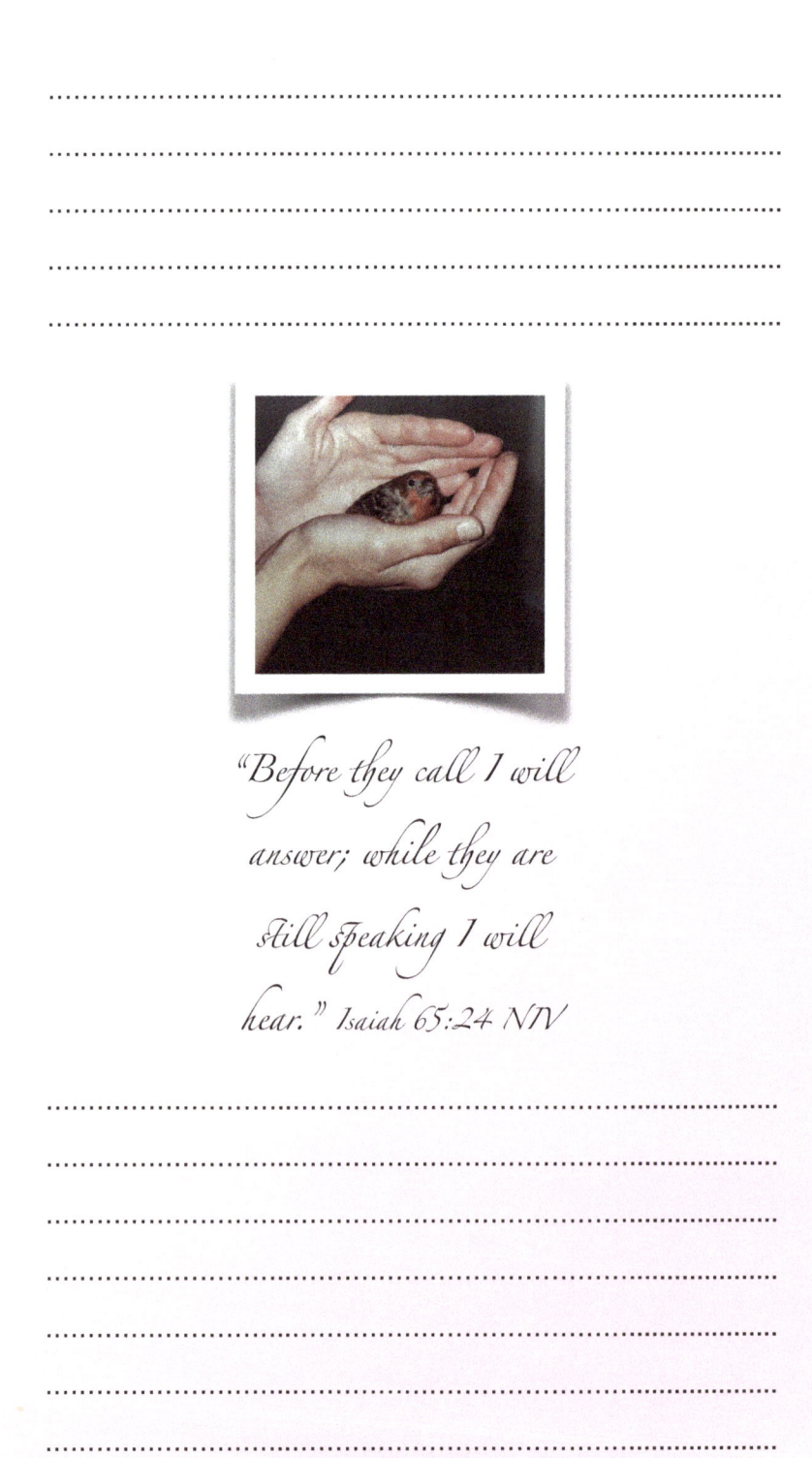

"Before they call I will answer; while they are still speaking I will hear." Isaiah 65:24 NIV

Soul's Introspection

I love the illustration of dawn, as a daily reminder that the Lord breaks the night's darkness with the sun. Out of the horizon its rays, rise. It's like a symbol of His resurrection power on display, daily. How does this give you hope, to carry on, today?

"For once you were darkness, but now you are light in the Lord; walk as children of Light [live as those who are native-born to the Light] (for the fruit [the effect, the result] of the Light consists in all goodness and righteousness and truth) ..." Ephesians 5:8-9 AMP

....
....
....
....
....
....
....
....
....
....
....
....
....
....
....
....
....
....
....
....
....

Prayer, is the sweetest gift that we can give another human being. Whether known or unknown, it can connect us, heal, encourage, bring courage, faith, hope, and even produce Salvation. Who needs this sweetest blessing from your soul, unto the throne? Who might be lifted out of darkness, into God's heavenly light?

Below, share your requests with God.

....
....
....
....
....
....
....
....
....
....
....
....

"Why am I praying like this? Because I know you will answer me, O God! Yes, listen as I pray." Psalm 17:6 TLB

The wee hours, especially at 12:00am or 3:00am, are known as specific times that God speaks to His children. I often ask the Lord, who needs to be remembered? Who has a need, that only He knows about? Who needs to know Him and His love?

....
....
....
....
....

I have found some of my richest times of communion with my Savior in these precious moments—called, the "watch hours." If you are awakened—will you ask the Lord to bring His light into the darkness, so that you can be His servant, and His prayer warrior?

"I rise before dawn and cry for help; I wait for Your words. My eyes anticipate the night watches, so that I may meditate on Your word." Psalm 119:147-148 NASB

....
....
....
....
....
....
....
....
....
....
....
....

Write out your favorite verse about meditation, then record a fresh insight about why it is special to you. Did God speak anything new into your heart?

....
....
....
....
....
....
....
....
....

If I am lying awake "worrying" I turn these concerns into prayers. How might this approach help you rely on God?

> Out of darkness, we wake from our slumber. Out of darkness, we rise, to see light shine through our rooms and upon the earth. And every day, we get to experience the Light of the World in some new faceted way, as He lives and moves and breathes upon all creation.

....

....

....

....

....

....

....

....

....

....

....

....

....

....

....

"The faithful love of the Lord never ends! His mercies never cease. Great is his faithfulness; his mercies begin afresh each morning." Lamentations 3:22-23 NLT

Praise—Out of Darkness

This is a freeform space, designed for you to write a few "Thank You's" to the Lord. It's a place for you to express some praise or some need or simply "speak your heart" to the One Who loves you, and knows you, completely.

Has God delivered you from darkness? Physically, perhaps from illness, an accident, or a particularly difficult time in your life? Emotionally, from a time of pain or grief? Or spiritually, to make you His child? Expressing gratitude, brings God joy.

From darkness, we are delivered into the light of His love. If nothing comes immediately to mind … take a few moments to meditate upon the miracle that is, darkness into dawn. Or thank Him for this new day and the breath that fills your lungs.

....

....

....

....

....

....

God's silence can sometimes be perceived as "darkness." Yet I have often found that in these times, He is still speaking ... through His Word, creation, through worship and as I continue to praise Him. How can silence be a gift or a weapon—in a relationship, with others, or toward God?

"Night is almost over, and day will soon appear. We must stop behaving as people do in the dark and be ready to live in the light." Romans 13:12 CEV

....

....

....

....

....

....

....

....

....

....

....

....

....

....

....

....

Embracing Light

*"Praise the Lord, my soul.
Lord my God, you are very great;
you are clothed with splendor and majesty.*

*He made the moon to mark the seasons,
and the sun knows when to go down.
You bring darkness, it becomes night, ...*

*I will sing to the Lord all my life;
I will sing praise to my God as long as I live."*

Psalm 104: 1-2, 19-20a, & 33 NIV

Above, the Lord is being described as clothed in majesty. Heaven's lights could be depicted in much the same way. How do these things of creation display God's warmth to body, mind, and soul?

....

....

....

....

....

....

....

....

....

....

....

Notice how the sun highlighted this seagull? I find it amazing how God touches all creation with His illumination. What are you noticing?

"Your word is a lamp to my feet and a light to my path."
Psalm 119:105 NKJV

....
....
....
....
....
....
....
....
....

The Lord is my Light and my Salvation.

The Solace of Light

- Do you long for a place of solace?
- A place to pause and rest, not just your body, but your heart and mind, as well?
- Do you seek a place of joy, peace, a perfect communion?

There's something magical about light. From the first rays of dawn to the way it reflects and changes over the landscape, to the way it illuminates every shadow, to the way it embraces our hearts. ... We are drawn to it, enveloped by it, and given warmth, comfort, hope and peace, from its ethereal glow. We can even experience the feeling of God's love through its existence.

"Because of God's tender mercy, the morning light from heaven is about to break upon us, to give light ... and to guide us to the path of peace." Luke 1:78-79 NLT

Dawn unfolds upon the horizon.
Pastel shades of jewel-like tones explode like Iolite,
Pale Ruby and tranquil Amethyst, to illumine the coming day.
Upwardly, cool Topaz moves in the sky toward its zenith.
And whether you have noticed the beauty or not,
Light has embraced you.
It has touched you, your home, and your environment.

How has light proven to be a solace in your life?

....
....
....
....
....
....
....
....
....
....
....
....
....
....
....
....
....

Enveloping Light

Light surrounds us in every 24 hour period. We open our eyes to alarm clocks, which project the time in LED images. We wake to dawn, clear and bright, or smoky, yet it is still illuminating. We are exposed to lamps and work lights, computer and phone screens and other devices that display and filter, light. Early and late hours, are filled with car lights, street lights. And the night-time, is lit with the moon and stars, glow.

These lights, both natural and man-made, touch each one of us, every day. There are colored lights to celebrate every holiday and festival throughout the year. There are atmospheric lights which we use in our homes to calm our spaces and hearts. We use paint colors to create the illusion of light, and magnify how it reflects through a room. Light moves to form shadows, dances upon water, and glistens from heaven.

> ....
>
> ....
>
> ....

Light, perhaps more than any other of God's creations, is His communication of love to mankind. Because it touches us in so many forms, it's a wonderful way to imagine God's embrace, personally.

Dear Lord,

May Your Light dawn in our souls, today,
To remind us that we need,
Some time in stillness and meditation, with You.

Helps us see our need for the quiet,
And some rest, from all that we have to do.

May we seek to give You praises,
And speak the things upon our hearts.

....
....
....
....
....
....
....
....
....
....
....
....

For in this space, ...
Perhaps, Your grace,
Will dawn, ...
To let Your love,
Shine through. Amen.   ....

Let God's love embrace you today,
Through every source of light,
That you see.
Try to count how many forms,
Are in your daily, routine. ...
Then thank Him,
For the man-made,
And the natural ones,
That only He could provide.
But for each one that you observe,
May you take a moment,
To feel His affection and care.
For it reaches down from heaven,
To touch earth,
And your beating heart,
—Always.

Note your observations:

....
....
....
....
....
....
....
....
....
....
....
....
....

Light is not put under a basket. Instead, it's placed in a candlestand, so that it offers its illumination.

Lord, may my soul glow with Your love and grace. Let me not be ashamed to share the truth of Who You are to me, to those around me. Amen.

Soul's Introspection

"Can I go anywhere apart from Your Spirit? Is there anywhere I can go to escape Your watchful presence? If I go up into heaven, You are there. If I make my bed in the realm of the dead, You are there. If I ride on the wings of morning, if I make my home in the most isolated part of the ocean, even then You will be there to guide me; Your right hand will embrace me, for You are always there. ...

....
....
....
....
....
....
....

... Even if I am afraid and think to myself, 'There is no doubt that the darkness will swallow me, the light around me will soon be turned to night,' You can see in the dark, for it is not dark to Your eyes. For You the night is just as bright as the day. Darkness and light are the same to Your eyes." Psalm 139:7-12 VOICE

....
....
....
....
....
....
....
....
....

Light embraces us in many forms.

Earth and heaven are filled with it, and glow with light. It shines from our eyes, from our souls. And the kaleidoscope can teach us a few lessons.

There's something about this object that draws young and old alike, because …
- Light transforms it.
- We participate in forming the art.
- It's different every time we pick it up.

Perhaps God uses every source of light, and the dance of light and shadow, to embrace us 24 hours a day—with His love.

Will you look for the warmth of the Son in every light source that surrounds you?

....
....
....
....
....
....
....
....
....
....
....
....
....

You are loved.

....
....
....
....
....
....
....
....
....

"Light brings every kind of goodness, right living, and truth."
Ephesians 5:9 ICB

....
....
....
....
....
....
....
....
....
....

You are cherished.

Stillness:

"Yahweh your God is among you, a warrior who saves. He will rejoice over you with gladness. He will bring you quietness with His love. He will delight in you with shouts of joy." Zephaniah 3:17 HCSB

Stillness—
means to stop all movement, to be silent, to live with a sense of peace and contentment, to possess a calm spirit that is filled with joy, to trust God—completely.

These moments in His company, become as much a part of our spirit, as He is with us.

If we become still, God can create room to show us His beauty. He can speak in a whisper—softly or loudly—to communicate to our inner being. And He can give us glimpses of "still waters"—that touch our lives—not only for a moment, but linger for all eternity.

Stillness, implies quieting our minds, our hearts, etc., but it also means including some version of solitude so that we can worship, which helps us halt our restlessness. These, encourage us to come before God with our wishes, our everything—surrendered.

When we learn to delight in the Lord—in stillness—He often brings us into spaces that stop us in our tracks.

These, allow us to see, hear, and know Him. Here, He is exalted. Here, we learn to know Him—intimately, intricately and personally—as we walk with Him, in every season.

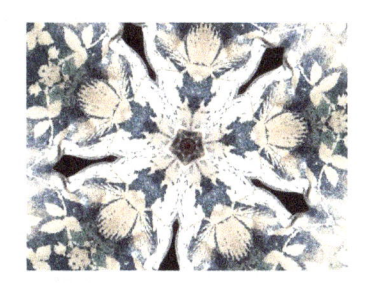

When is a time, that God has rewarded your moment of stillness with a special insight, an answered prayer, or revealed a special lesson from His Word?

Below, draw or attach a special photo, that depicts your favorite time of day.

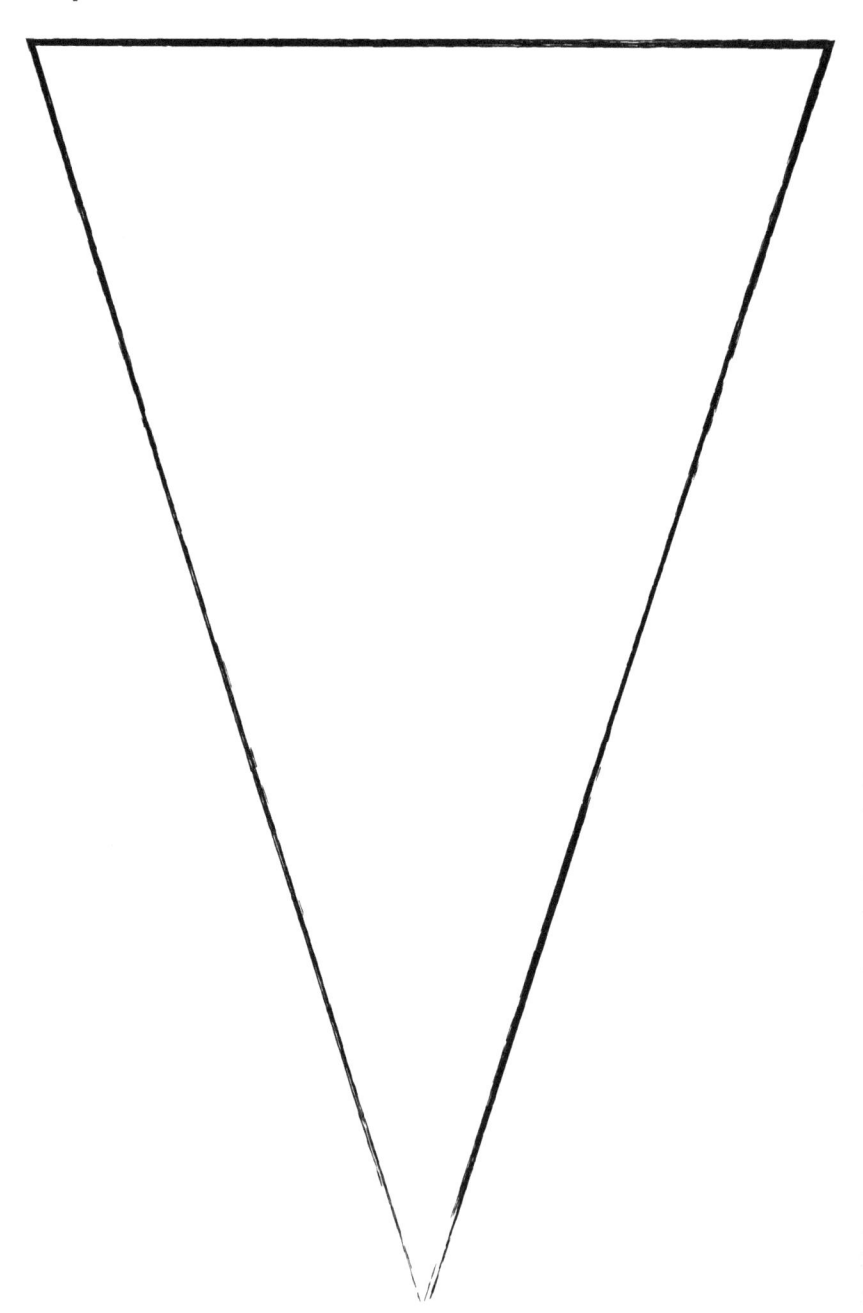

What about your artwork or picture, speaks to your heart?

Take a step of faith and let God, be God. Stillness, does not always mean inactivity. It means staying in communion with Him, His Word, but doing what you know to be obedient, and then recording what He does on your behalf. That's how we mature in trust, and believe that He's changing us, day by day.

Walking with God, means that you are never alone.

....
....
....
....
....
....
....
....
....
....
....
....
....
....
....
....
....
....

Come, absorb the quiet,
Let Me, still the riot,
Of your thoughts,
Of your concerns.

Come, absorb the stillness,
Let Me, fill your emptiness,
I'll remove,
Your doubt and fears.

Come, absorb the solitude,
Bring me a gentle, open attitude,
And I will draw near,
To speak to your soul.

The Lantern

Upon the wall,
Hangs a scroll-work lantern.
Inside it,
Stands a candle,
With a wick,
Of wax-coated thread.
With a single match,
A spark,
Explodes,
Into a moment of light.
The two join,
To create a flame.
And inside,
The interior of the globe,
Is lit,
To shine,
To reflect its radiance,
Throughout the room.

Dear Jesus, may this process be duplicated within my soul. Amen.

How can you let your light shine, uniquely, to give God glory?

……………………………….

……………………………….

……………………………….

……………………………….

……………………………….

……………………………….

……………………………….

……………………………….

……………………………….

………………………………….

………………………………….

………………………………….

………………………………….

………………………………….

………………………………….

………………………………….

………………………………….

………………………………….

Dear Jesus,
May a flame of Your love be likewise, duplicated, within my soul. For as I surrender, not only my heart, but my every dream and hope and goal, may You transform each, into the spark of faith. Amen.

"Bless the Lord, O my soul! O Lord my God, You are very great: You are clothed with honor and majesty, who cover Yourself with light as with a garment, who stretch out the heavens like a curtain." Psalm 104:1-2 NKJV

Light separates darkness. The sun and moon each govern our day and night. God gave them their own spaces to illumine and uses them to mark our seasons. How does this display His faithfulness and care?

....
....
....
....
....
....
....
....
....
....
....
....

God's grace shines in and through every shadow, to remind us that He is near.

Through the Veil

The mist nestled,
O're the fields, the plains.
The clouds hung heavily,
In the sky.
Here and there, they met,
To obscure one's view.
But even through the veil—
I saw You, Adonai.

If you feel a mist rest upon your mind, or clouds lower o're your soul—seek Adonai. If a veil happens to fill your eyes and runs down your cheeks, reach out toward God's grace. He is near, aware, and His love will always shine through—every shadow—to cut through the gloom and drench your heart in purest light.

"When he sneezes, the sunlight sparkles like lightning across the vapor droplets. His eyes glow like sparks." Job 41:18 TLB

....

....

....

....

....

....

....

Dear Lord, I invite You to wash Your light into every space of my home, my heart, my life, my thoughts, actions and deeds. Remove any shadow and let Your Spirit glow, dance, and be reflected from my very soul. May every space that I enter, display something of Your radiance. For it is Your light that transforms, renews, cleanses, illuminates—one soul at a time—until the world knows You, as its Source, the Son. Amen.

....

....

....

....

....

....

....

....

....

"Every good gift and every perfect gift is from above, and comes down from the Father of lights, with whom there is no variation or shadow of turning." James 1:17 NKJV

....

....

....

....

....

....

....

....

....

....

....

....

....

....

....

....

....

....

....

Jesus, thank You for the sunrise and sunset that are filled with such varied hues. As You wash the sky in watercolors, I am drawn to Your creativity. I want to know You, more nearly and dearly. I know that my life's plan, is being drawn with loving-kindness. Amen.

"May the God of hope fill you with all joy and peace in believing [through the experience of your faith] that by the power of the Holy Spirit you will abound in hope and overflow with confidence in His promises."
Romans 15:13 AMP

God holds hope as a gift, as light, to touch your mind, heart, and life.

Crystal Rain

Out of this corner of darkest rooftop, shone blue sky.
From the skylight, hung crystal droplets.
To my eye, the glass dewdrops,
appeared as rain.

Dear Jesus, let your love rain down upon me, in the darkest moments of confusion, fear or doubt. Let your light and hope and peace surround me, until I see only Your crystal-clear nearness. May Your Spirit descend like dewdrops, so that my mind and body feel as though a soothing shower has infused me with strength. For here, I learn to trust You. Here, I see You more clearly. Here, the embrace of Your loving-kindness comes into focus, as the cares of this world fade into obscurity. Amen.

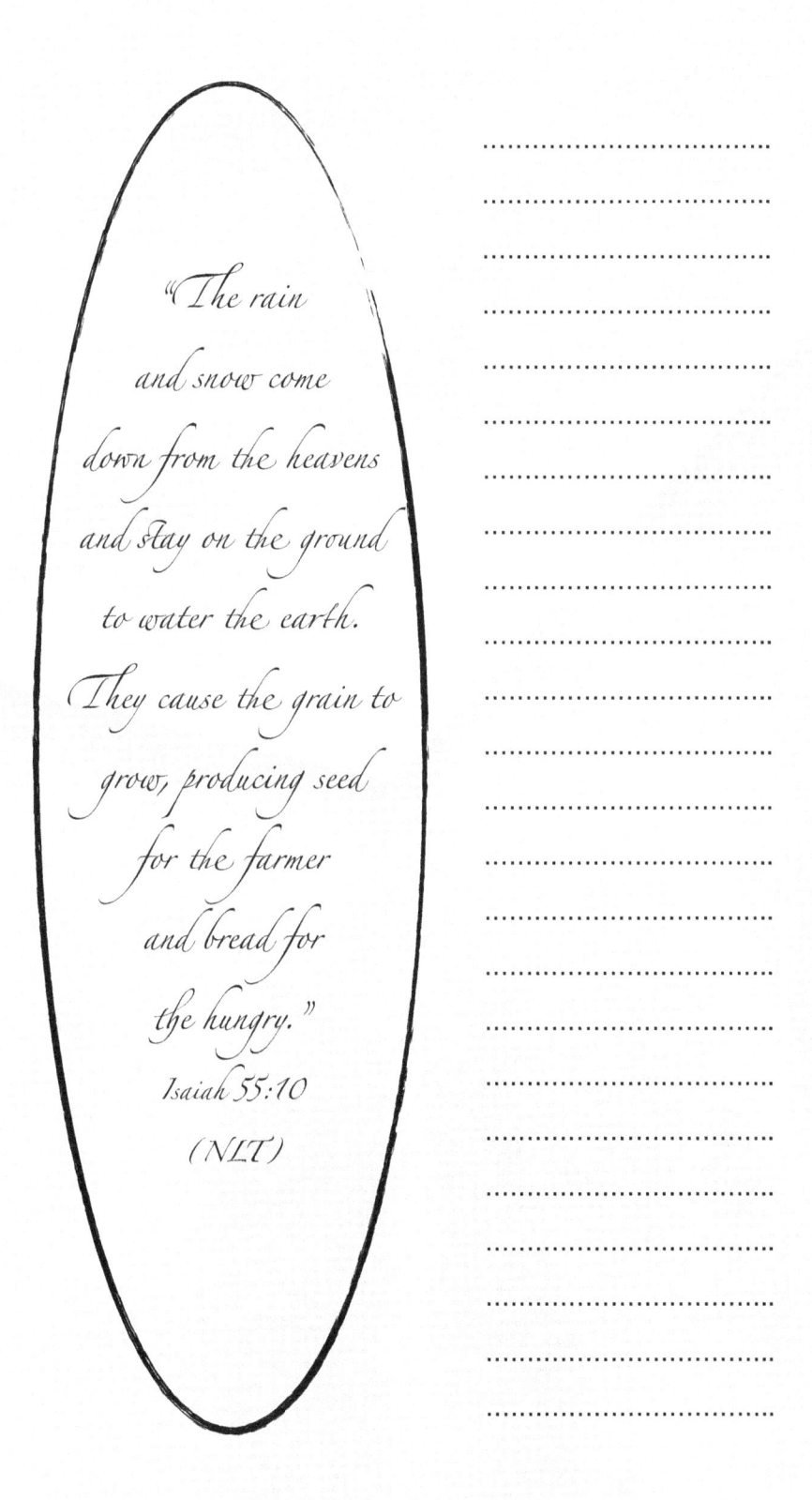

> "The rain and snow come down from the heavens and stay on the ground to water the earth. They cause the grain to grow, producing seed for the farmer and bread for the hungry."
> Isaiah 55:10 (NLT)

*God's love ... covers your past ... anoints
today ... and stretches forth, o're your future. How
does this thought, encourage you, today?*

The Lord is your guiding Light.

....
....
....
....
....
....
....
....

He has a plan and a purpose for your life. Have you asked the Lord for His Will and guidance, to find both?

....
....
....
....
....
....
....
....
....
....
....

"Understanding your word brings light to the minds of ordinary people."
Psalm 119:130 CEV

A Fresh Canvas

With each dawn, comes the ability to let the mistakes of yesterday, go; let the lessons, rise. It opens with hope, because it signifies that if we are here, alive—then You are not finished with us—and we are meant to do something, contribute something to our world. It means that we can lend a hand, spread some joy or encouragement, or shine a light of Your truth to every corner of our workplace, playspace, and community.

The very blessing of opening our eyes, and taking a breath into our lungs, should be miracle enough to propel us, to see this day as a starting place. It's a way of motivating us. We may not be where we want to be, but we have the chance to grow, learn, seek You, and let Your love infiltrate our hearts a little more each day.

How might viewing each new day in this fashion, change the arrival of each? Would it affect your attitude? Would you cherish each one as a gift?

"My heart is confident in you, O God; my heart is confident. No wonder I can sing your praises! Wake up, my heart! Wake up, O lyre and harp! I will wake the dawn with my song." Psalm 57:7-8 NLT

....
....
....
....
....
....
....
....
....
....
....
....
....
....
....
....
....

"Seek the Lord and his strength, seek his face continually." 1 Chronicles 16:11 KJV

Look Up, Out, Down, ... and Around

Look out, to the horizon,
To where the sun begins to shine.

Look up, into the heavens,
To the glorious sky, above.

Look down, at the shells on the seashore,
To the tiny-miracles in your hand.

Look around to see creation,
All the beauty He has made.

Look out, to the horizon,
To where the Son begins to shine.

....
....
....
....
....
....

So look up, look out, look down and all around; for everything that we can see and touch, and even imagine, is designed so that we recognize God's hand print, and so that we give Him our highest praise!

Jesus stilled the waves; let Him bring solace to your circumstance.

When have you needed to rely on God to be the island of your soul? When has His light reflected to declare you as His own?

....
....
....
....
....
....
....
....
....
....
....
....
....
....
....
....
....
....
....
....
....
....
....
....

A Glimpse into Heaven

The image before me, made me feel like I was being given a glimpse into heaven. The way the sun was coming from behind the clouds, the different shades of blue and gray in the sky, all formed this collage to make me pause. As sunlight lit each cloud and seemed to dance with the close of day, my mind filled with God's grandeur.

In that opening, that time and space, it was like God's love poured through it. I hope it appears that way to you also. Because His love is grander, bigger, wider, fuller, and deeper than my camera can capture, or your mind can comprehend.

Can you see it? Can you feel it?

....

....

....

....

....

....

....

"The Lord bless you, and keep you; the Lord make His face shine on you, and be gracious to you; the Lord lift up His countenance on you, and give you peace."
Numbers 6:24-26
(NASB)

May the glow of His love rest upon you, and may you sense His ray of hope, coming through any cloud in your life.

....
....
....
....
....
....
....
....
....
....
....
....
....
....
....
....
....
....
....
....

"He covers the heavens with clouds, sends down the showers, and makes the green grass grow in mountain pastures." Psalm 147:8 TLB

The Light of God's Grace

I loved walking into this scene on the backside of the Rocky Mountain range, in Colorado. It was late afternoon, and the sun was at its zenith. The mountain and the trees were held in shadow, yet the rays glistened downward from a crystal blue sky dotted with billowy clouds.

God's love and light illumine every hurt, every past mistake, every illness, any area where we feel lacking. His grace can cover any sin, any fear, any worry, to lift our eyes and focus onto His radiance.

Share with the Lord your greatest area of shadow, and write a prayer asking for His light to touch it.

....
....
....
....
....
....
....

*Darkness cannot overtake the soul
which has Jesus' Spirit living within.*

*Jesus says, "I will never leave you or forsake you."
(Hebrews 13:5)*

Evening and Morning

There are some scholars, who feel we have our day and night, reversed. We look at a day, as beginning—with the sun rising upon the horizon. Yet in Genesis, a few translations actually state evening and morning, created a day. Why am I pointing out this distinction? Because we may see each 24 hour period, in an entirely new light.

How might the idea that evening begins our day, help you get a deeper, more energizing rest? How might your daytime hours become more productive, if you saw them as the follow-on to restoration, instead of as a reward for a stress-filled schedule?

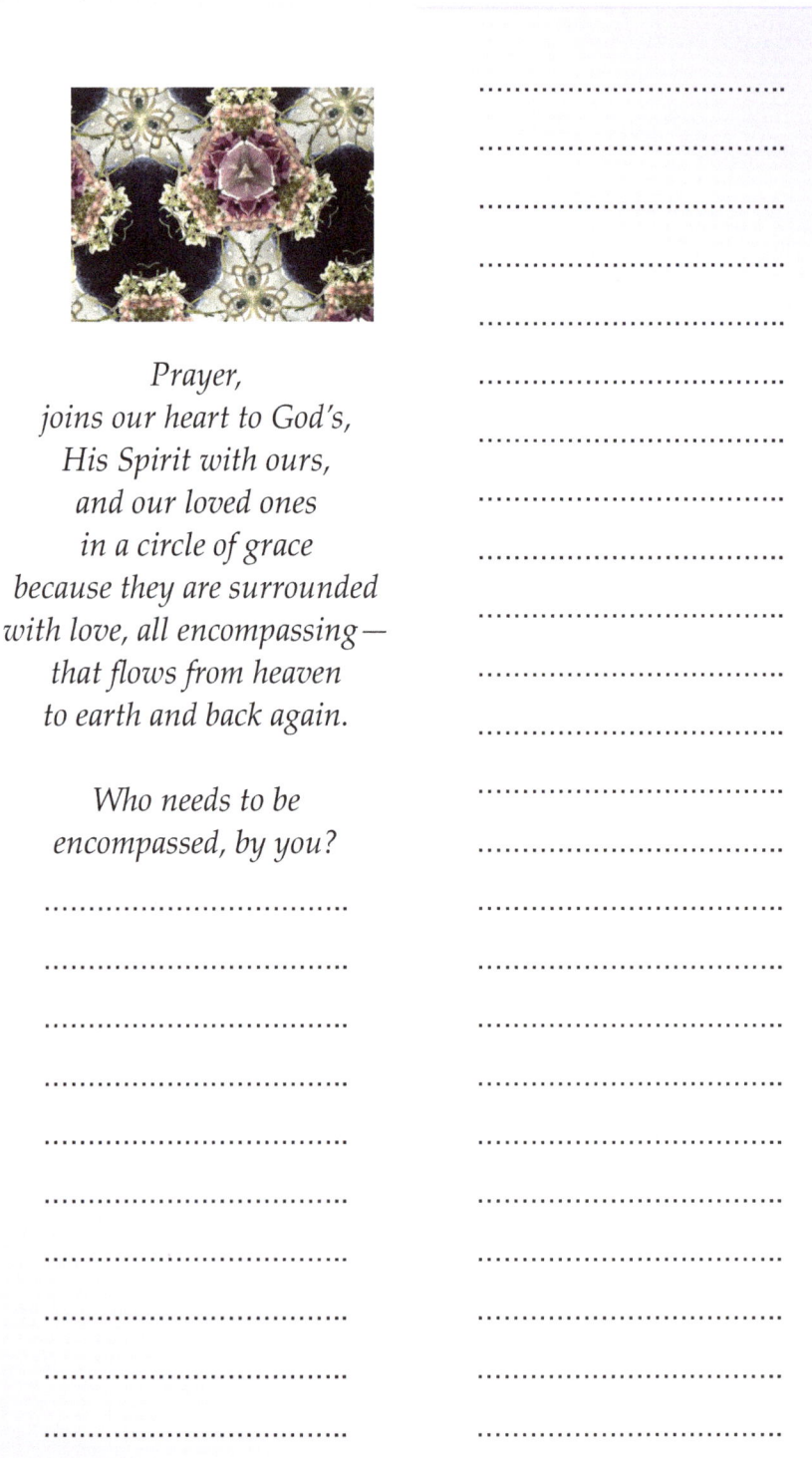

*Prayer,
joins our heart to God's,
His Spirit with ours,
and our loved ones
in a circle of grace
because they are surrounded
with love, all encompassing—
that flows from heaven
to earth and back again.*

*Who needs to be
encompassed, by you?*

Soul's Introspection

Dear Lord, teach us to see every form of light as a hug coming from Your throne, to envelop our hearts with Your love. Amen.

Below is room for your meditations about God's embracing light:

....
....
....
....
....
....
....
....
....
....
....
....
....
....
....
....
....
....

Prisms on Ice

Upon the crackled ice,
As twilight fell,
Sunset left a trail,
—Of prisms.
They danced,
And lit these floating islands,
To glisten,
In the eventide,
That swiftly descended.
Around them,
Flowed open water.
—All combined,
To swish beauty, over the sky and sea.

....
....
....
....
....
....
....
....
....
....

- When you feel "at sea" ... is Jesus your anchor?
- Does His light shine from within, so that His love is reflected into all that you do and say?
- When the winds of hurt assail you, do you seek the Son for warmth, healing and grace?

> *Trust God —not when all else fails— but each new morning. Then, you'll know that He'll carry you through, every decision, every trial, every joy, through everything that comes your way. That's how you'll see God's faithfulness as a testimony of love.*

Record some of the ways that God has shown you His care, love and provision.

....
....
....
....
....
....
....
....
....
....
....
....
....
....
....
....
....
....
....
....
....
....

Softly and Loudly

There is a hush that enters,
    When the sun has fallen.
        The colors draw out, and up,
            O're the atmosphere.
                In the solitude, I find the silence,
            Speaks loudest,
        That my God, is near.

Twilight, feels like earth is saying its prayers for the night. It brings its final offerings of beauty and grace before the King. Quietly, humbly, it is shaded in peace. With gentleness, it seems to sing a hymn of praise to the Creator. The very atmosphere changes and becomes calm. Yet it speaks to my soul, clearly, loudly: "The Lord reigns. He is ever present. He is in the midst of the earth. He cares about you, me, about all that He has made."

What's your soft request? What's your loud declaration?

....
....
....
....
....
....
....
....
....
....
....
....
....
....
....
....
....
....
....
....
....
....
....

> "From the rising of the sun to its setting, the name of the Lord is to be praised."
> Psalm 113:3 (NASB)

"The city does not need the sun or the moon to shine on it, for the glory of God gives it light, and the Lamb is its lamp."
Revelation 21:23 NIV

....
....
....
....
....
....
....
....
....
....

God does not sleep or slumber. May this truth bring you peace when you're lying awake in the night; call upon His name!

....
....
....
....
....
....
....
....
....
....
....
....
....
....
....
....
....
....
....
....

"Then, oh then, your light will break out like the warm, golden rays of a rising sun; in an instant, you will be healed. Your rightness will precede and protect you; the glory of the Eternal will follow and defend you." Isaiah 58:8 VOICE

Praise—Embracing Light

Whether you are greeted by the colorful illumination of an alarm clock, a bathroom light, the sun streaming through the window, or see it reflected upon a wintery landscape ... light, is all around us.
It shines 'round about us, from all directions.

What are some of the light sources for which you are grateful? What might a "Thank You" note look like, sound like, to the Light of the World, if you counted every source of light that you encounter on a given day? Which one(s) would be most pro-foundly, missed, if they were to disappear?

"You are the Eternal, the only One. The skies are Your work alone—You made the heavens above those skies and the stars that fill them. You made the earth and everything upon it, the seas and all that lives within their depths. Your creation lives and is sustained by You, and those who dwell in the heavens, fall down before You and worship." Nehemiah 9:6 VOICE

Under a Canopy of Stars

Triangles, facets, geometric shapes—form within a circular tube—to create star-like images. Suddenly a toy—fills the daytime with God's glory—bursting, shining, glittering and sparkly right before our eyes. In it, we can see our Creator's creativity—in every hour of the day/night.

Will you let the stars remind you that God's a bit starry-eyed over you?

....
....
....
....
....
....
....
....
....
....
....
....
....
....

God calls each star by name. The moon changes its shape nightly, marking time, marking the tides. Under a canopy of velvet sky, His glory, glistens, silently, yet speaks volumes to the heart, that beholds Him, as Lord.

North Star

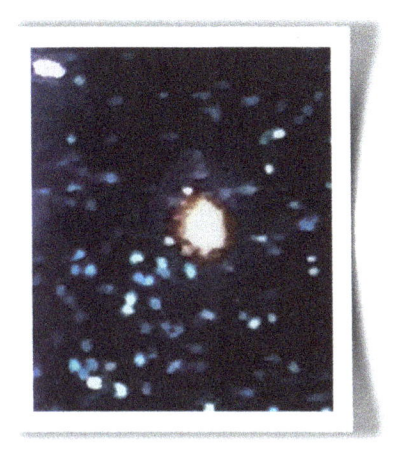

The telescope, much like the kaleidoscope, magnifies not just the stars of space, but brings us into a sanctuary of solitude. Here, we find ourselves alone with the audience of One, in a private moment of communion, to ponder with wonder, His glory.

In the solitude of night, I can often feel God's presence so nearly, so dearly. I can get my bearing and hear His voice, with a clarity that the noises of the daytime hours, do not allow. So if you need to hear His voice, try looking up at the sky.

How is God, your "north star?"

....
....
....
....
....
....
....
....
....
....

*May you find rest for your body, mind and soul,
before the audience of One, Who is our perfect Guide.*

Soul's Introspection

"I look up at your macro-skies, dark and enormous, your handmade sky-jewelry, moon and stars mounted in their settings. Then I look at my micro-self and wonder, why do you bother with us? Why take a second look our way? Yet we've so narrowly missed being gods, bright with Eden's dawn light. You put us in charge of your handcrafted world, repeated to us your Genesis-charge, made us lords of sheep and cattle, even animals out in the wild, birds flying and fish swimming, whales singing in the ocean deeps." Psalm 8:3-8 MSG

....
....
....
....
....
....
....
....
....
....
....
....
....
....
....

"The moon strides through her phases, marking seasons as she goes. The sun hides at his appointed time, and with the darkness You bring, so comes night—when the prowling animals of the forest move about." Psalm 104:19-20 VOICE

As Jewels

Lord, are the stars,
Your version of diamonds,
With perfect cut, color and clarity?
Is the moon,
One large pearl,
With its luster,
And iridescent luminosity?
Are the planets and galaxies,
Shaped and faceted,
Like precious jewels—
Hanging—
Yet, mounted by Your Holy hand?

....
....
....
....
....
....
....
....
....

"To Him who made the great lights,
for His lovingkindness is everlasting:
The sun to rule by day, for His
lovingkindness is everlasting,
the moon and stars to rule by night,
for His loving-kindness is
everlasting." Psalm 136:7-9 NASB

You know my every thought—yet You long for my voice to praise You, to worship, to bring my needs and requests before Your throne, in a gift of submission. It is this holy conversation that joins earth and heaven—time and space—for all eternity. It is a promise to my soul to know that You are always listening, attentive to my first cry, or utterance of joy, or greatest need.

- Bring our Praises and Petitions: Philippians 4:6
- Pray for others, & offer prayer with joy: Philippians 1:3-6
- The Moon and Stars display His loving-kindness: Psalm 136:7-9
- Lift up your eyes to the Creator of the Stars: Isaiah 40:26
- The Lord hears our voice and supplications: Psalm 116:1

On that Night of Miracles

On that night of miracles,
The wise men followed a star.
It lit the heavens,
To pave the way for worship,
And bearing gifts to the Christ Child.
It rested above the little town of Bethlehem,
Where Jesus lay swaddled in the manger.
And on any given night,
We can remember,
By simply going outside,
Into the twilight,
To behold His majesty in creation.

Have you ever chosen a star as your very own, to wish upon? Pray upon? To think upon—as possibly the one that appeared and has remained—to lift our eyes to the Lord's divinity? Have you ever thanked God for all of the gifts that He has bestowed upon your life: breath, each new day, His faithful provision and care? And have you ever offered Him gifts: tithes, offerings, your time, talents, love and adoration?

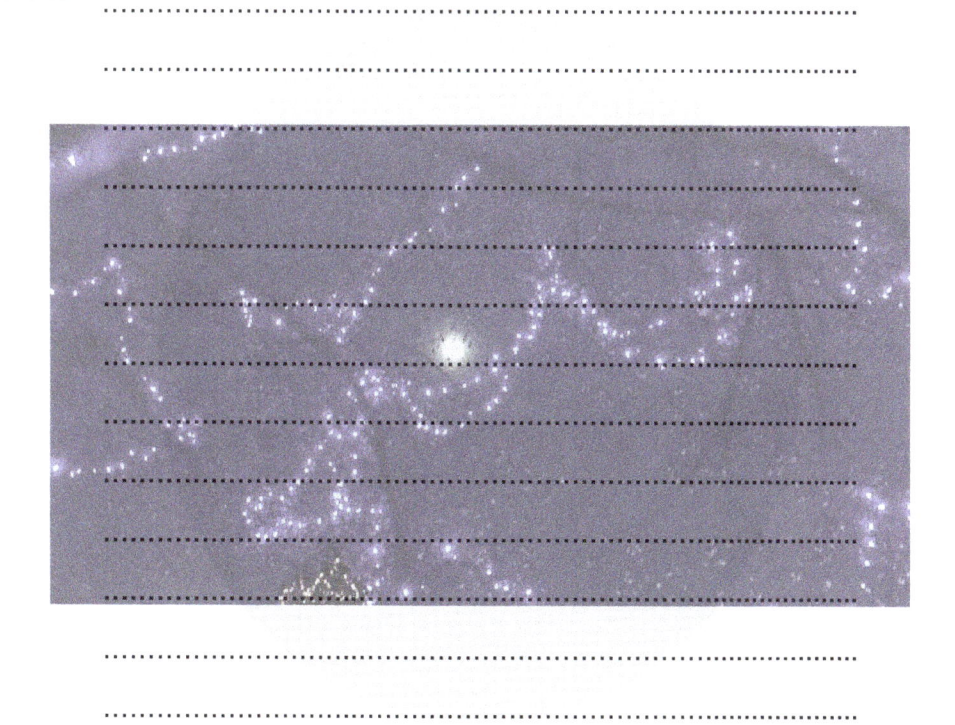

....

....

....

....

....

....

....

....

....

....

....

....

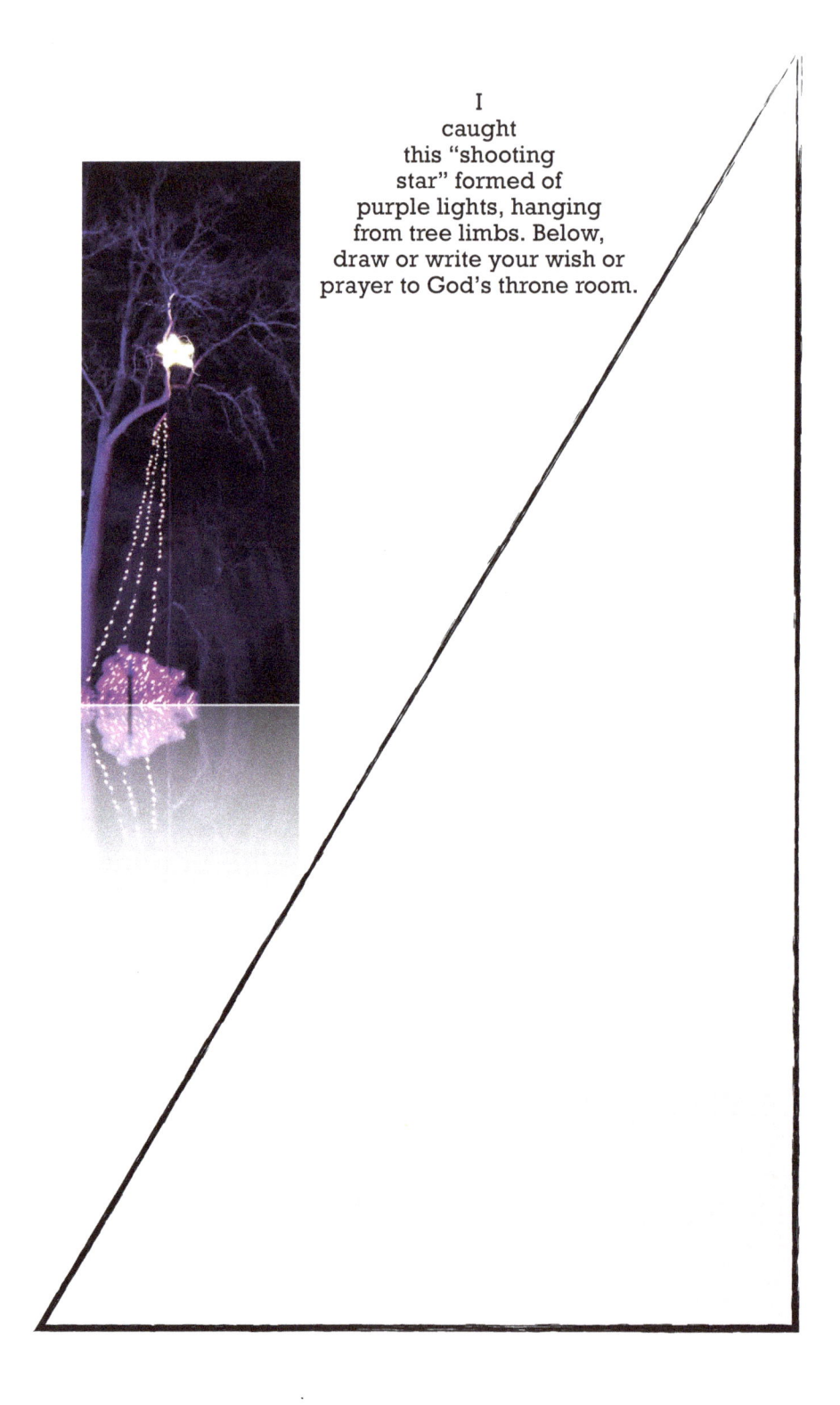

I caught this "shooting star" formed of purple lights, hanging from tree limbs. Below, draw or write your wish or prayer to God's throne room.

The stars are held in place by God's power — He can take care of you.

Tell Jesus your secrets, He'll never betray you.

The Full Moon's View of Earth

The full moon this evening made me wonder: What would we be able to do for God's kingdom—if we saw ourselves as He sees us? In seeing its perfection, I thought ... this is how our Father views our heart, if we have received Jesus as Lord and Savior. In Him, nothing is missing, we are made whole. So as you gaze at the night sky, ask Him for a dream. And know that whatever He places in your heart, is perfect. One perfect moon, One perfect Lord; it's one perfect night to dream! What's yours?

One Autumn evening we participated in a moon-walk. It was amazing to behold the night's grandeur unfolding, as if God was unrolling a scroll upon the landscape. How does the nightly show of His handiwork reflect His presence in your life?

"Even among the heavenly bodies, there is a different level of brilliance: the sun shines differently than the moon, the moon differently than the stars, and the stars themselves differ in their brightness."
1 Corinthians 15:41 VOICE

"Those who are wise will shine like the brightness of the heavens, and those who lead many to righteousness, like the stars forever and ever."
Daniel 12:3 (NIV)

Have you ever gone home, met a friend or loved one ... and were greeted with "stars in their eyes?" That's how God looks at you —always. His love shines upon you, constantly. It is like a meteor shower, filled with grace. How does that make you feel?

....
....
....
....
....
....
....
....
....
....
....
....
....
....
....
....
....
....

God's eye is on the smallest of creatures—remember that, when you feel alone, tired, or insignificant in this big world.

"Your love and kindness are forever; your truth is as enduring as the heavens." Psalm 89:2 TLB

....
....
....
....
....
....
....
....
....
....
....
....
....
....
....
....
....
....
....
....

"[May the people fear You] for as long as the sun shines, as long as the moon rises in the night sky, throughout the generations." Psalm 72:5 VOICE

Oh Galaxies of Heaven

> The moonbeam shines down,
> O're all the land.
> Light and shadow are formed,
> By His mighty hand.
> Right into the galaxy's path they ride,
> The glories of heaven are opened, wide.
> O Galaxies of Heaven,
> You leave me in awe,
> For you are but the footstool,
> Of Your Creator,
> My Lord, and All in All.

O Galaxies of Heaven, are but stardust in comparison to Who You are! Amen.

Twinkle Twinkle
His Eye of Love

Twinkle, Twinkle,
Little Star,
You help me remember,
That God is not very far,
From my presence,
Only a prayer away,
One word in request or worship,
And His ear is instantly,
Bent my way.
As I gaze into heaven,
It is You, I see,
My heavenly Father,
Ever, watching over me.

The moon and stars rise at His command, they obey at His voice, and twinkle at the touch of His fingers. If He can hold all of time and space in gravity, He can hold our concerns, our every need. Look up to the heavens, look into the eyes of the Father. Behold the One Who holds the answers, and Who holds you with eternal love—because He does. His love is like a canopy of blessing and peace.

The Lord is my Lantern — the guide of my path.

If you find a shooting star, what would be your wish? What would be your prayer?

> "You are like that illuminating light. Let your light shine everywhere you go, that you may illumine creation, so men and women everywhere may see your good actions, may see creation at its fullest, may see your devotion to Me, and may turn and praise your Father in heaven because of it." Matthew 5:16 (VOICE)

Space Between

You are ...
... the space-between,
... the sun and the moon,
... heaven and earth,
... pain and healing,
... cuts and scars,
... joy and happiness,
... peace and contentment.

May your heart be reminded that God knows you by name. He's whispering His nearness into the depths of your soul ... every day ... every night ... always!

Have you ever tried to count the stars above your head on a clear night? At what number did you lose count?

....
....
....
....
....
....
....
....
....
....
....
....
....

"He who made the Pleiades and Orion and changes deep darkness to morning. Who darkens the day into night. Who summons the water of the sea and pours it out on the face of the earth—Adonai is His Name." Amos 5:8 TLV

Since the stars number more than the grains of sand on the seashore ... are they reminders to us, of Your endless thoughts toward us, O God?

Moon through the Evergreens

As the moon shone through the evergreens, holiness brushed all of earth. With its anointing, my soul was touched to give God honor, on this treasured wintery night. Is yours?

....
....
....
....
....
....
....
....
....
....
....

"Yet in the light of day, the Eternal shows me His love. When night settles in and all is dark, He keeps me company—His soothing song, a prayerful melody to the True God of my life." Psalm 42:8 VOICE

Knowing God, by the Lights of Heaven

Father, we woke to a quarter-storybook-moon. It was visible, as the beginnings of dawn formed on the horizon, and I felt the nearness of Your presence.

Thank You, that as the moon and sun rise and set, Your love rotates around us, in a constant, never-ending circle of peace. I breathe in, and know that You are with me. I breathe out, and feel Your Spirit fill me with thanksgiving. Amen.

> *Lord,*
> *give us glimpses of who you've created*
> *us to be, so that we fulfill, at least in part,*
> *Your Will for us while we are on the earth.*
> *To do so, would be to bring You glory,*
> *today, and for all eternity. Amen.*
>
> *Have you ever asked the Lord for*
> *His specific vision for your life?*

Have you ever viewed the sun's rays, as one of the ways God is reaching out to you? This often happens after rain. How does this image encourage you during times of difficulty, or in the dark hours of night?

....
....
....
....
....
....
....
....
....
....
....
....
....
....
....
....
....

"Your constant love reaches above the heavens; your faithfulness touches the skies." Psalm 108:4 GNT

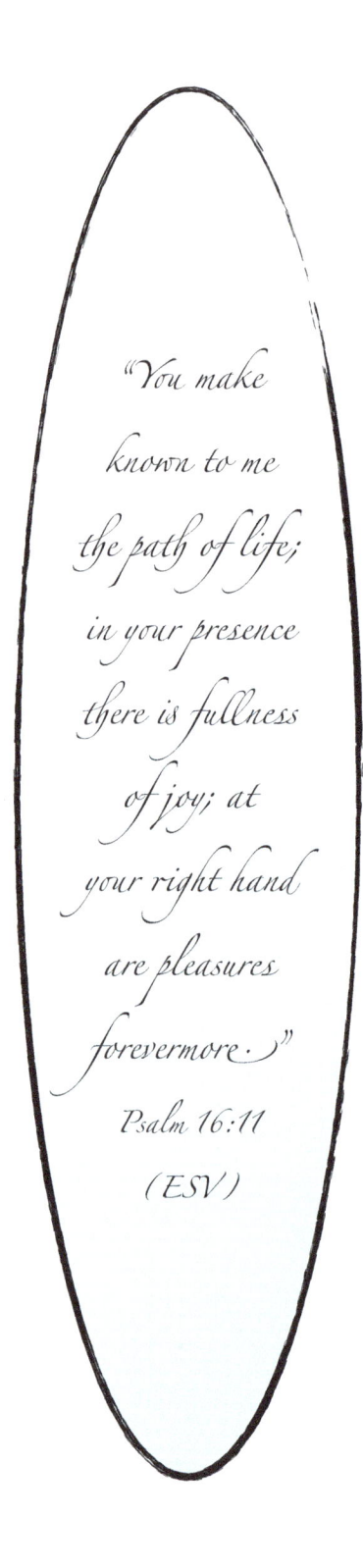

> "You make known to me the path of life; in your presence there is fullness of joy; at your right hand are pleasures forevermore."
> Psalm 16:11 (ESV)

Unfurl the Curtain

God unfurls a curtain,
Night falls into place.
The moon and stars,
Fill the sky and space.
The twilight is filled,
With a glittering field,
Myriad kinds of light,
To the shadows, yield.
God's power is displayed,
His might is arrayed,
For each of these,
Reflects the light of His soul.

....
....
....
....
....
....
....
....
....
....

Dear Lord,
    Unfurl the curtain of my heart. Plant Your seeds like the stars, until there is the glow of Your Spirit shining brightly, to show
                        my love for You.
                              Amen.

"And we have the prophetic word more fully confirmed, to which you will do well to pay attention as to a lamp shining in a dark place, until the day dawns and the morning star rises in your hearts."
...
2 Peter 1:19 (ESV)

Praise—Under a Canopy of Stars

Do you have a favorite star or constellation? Do you enjoy stargazing, wishing or praying, upon a certain starry host? What "Thank You's" fill your mind, when you consider that God has named each of these luminous, glittering orbs, individually? And that He cares for you, with the same intricate detail?

....
....
....
....
....
....
....
....

From the Inside, Out

A Kaleidoscope's exterior—may be fairly plain, or brightly colored and patterned. But from the inside, they explode with a profusion of images and changing scenes.

God lives on the inside of us (our hearts) to indwell the soul and transform body, mind and spirit—into surrendered followers that He treats as children—part of His family.

....
....
....
....
....
....
....
....
....

God fashioned your interior and your exterior with equal detail. Both work together, in perfect function to bring Him glory. We, like the kaleidoscope, display His love outwardly to Him and others, daily. Are you letting His Spirit perfect the design?

Pause

To pause, can mean to halt our steps, quiet our thoughts, to cease our activity, to turn off the noise.

In a spiritual sense, it means to focus-in on God's Spirit and His voice within our hearts. It's to notice the Lord's presence in the things He has made, and to have an awareness of His nearness.

Body, mind and soul are refreshed, when we stop and commune with the Lord. If we are quiet, we can absorb the sounds of nature; in stillness, we soak-in His Spirit's teaching; and in solitude, we discover that we are not alone, if we are trusting in the One True God.

....

....

....

These three: quiet, stillness and solitude, are the humble keys to knowing Jesus, in a sweeter, more profound way. But it takes discipline in order to achieve them. If we want a close walk with our Savior, we must stop our hectic pace, and bow before Him.

For it is through this precious fellowship, that our greatest battles are won. It is in this space, where we are taught directly by God. And it is here, that we learn the meaning of faith, and how to trust in our Abba Daddy.

For some, pausing, is out of their comfort zone. It's certainly incongruent with our culture. It goes against the grain of our too-busy-schedules and goal-oriented lives. Yet margin, peace and joy, are only achieved when we surrender to these gifts of God's grace.

> *"For God alone my soul waits in silence; from him comes my salvation." Psalm 62:1 ESV*

....

....

....

....

....

In what area is God asking you to "push pause?" In your schedule? In your work-life? In your commitments? Or in order to make time to meet with Him?

....
....
....
....
....
....
....
....
....
....
....
....
....
....
....
....
....
....
....
....

Dear Lord, I ask You to teach me how to pause. Sometimes I allow my to-do-list, to out prioritize my appointment with You. Convict me of this, because I know when I take time to put You first, everything will get done and You will give me strength for everything that is in Your Will. Amen.

A Sand Dollar is a wonderful illustration of God's invisible wonders, made visible. To me, this is proof that God creates all things with intricacy and the finest of detail. He cares for us, with this same degree of intimacy, also.

"And now God can always point to us as examples of how very, very rich his kindness is, as shown in all he has done for us through Jesus Christ. Because of his kindness, you have been saved through trusting Christ. And even trusting is not of yourselves; it too is a gift from God. Salvation is not a reward for the good we have done, so none of us can take any credit for it."
Ephesians 2:7-9 TLB

Like a Kaleidoscope

If you take a kaleidoscope,
In your hands,
And hold it up to an object,
It can change flowers,
Rocks or sand,
To create new patterns,
Making them come to life.

If God took a kaleidoscope,
To your soul,
And held it next to His image,
Would the pattern created,
Be colored by His love?
Have you been washed,
By His cleansing flood?
Would you be sparkling,
With His light?
Are you being transformed,
By day, by night?

Erosion's Treasure

As we have gone on day-trips to the beaches along Lake Michigan—we've noticed erosion—serious erosion. It's like the shoreline is being cut-away, sculpted, each time we travel there. Trees have been felled, uprooted. Sand, has been shifted. Areas that were once able to be walked upon, no longer have space to do so. The tide runs right up to the bank. In fact, the shoreline in some places now resemble cliffs.

....
....
....
....
....

Dear Jesus, when I feel worn down, battered, scared, tired ... please allow me to see a glimpse of the design You're creating, within. For when you show me even a piece of the internal workings, I am encouraged to trust. I am given faith to believe that the barren places will be filled; the hurts will be healed; I am given a firm foundation for the next wave. And I know that You will complete what You've begun, because You alone, control all that touches me. Amen.

....
....
....
....
....

Erosion, revealed the treasure of rocks as art, to my heart. God uses our pain, trials, and difficulties —to transform our inner being. We must trust Him with everything, knowing He is in control of the design.

Do you see God doing a version of this, in any area of your life?

> Which will you be,
> a waved-tossed sea?
> Or the one who prays,
> asks, and then believes?
> (See James 1:6-8)

....
....
....
....
....
....
....
....
....
....
....
....
....
....
....
....
....
....
....
....
....
....
....
....
....
....
....
....
....
....
....
....
....
....

What requests or concerns do you need to ask and then believe, into God's faithful care?

Lit by You

When twilight nestles,
On your horizon,
And storm clouds gather,
In your circumstances or mind …
Let God's embrace,
Wrap 'round you, like comfort.
He is the lantern,
The only true Light.
For as you draw close,
He will strike a flame inside you;
He'll place His Spirit's glow,
Like Living Water,
To display that you,
Are His marvelous show.

The lighthouse may be lit by man's genius, but the soul that holds the flame of God's Spirit, is a wonder indeed—let it shine forth—with His holiness.

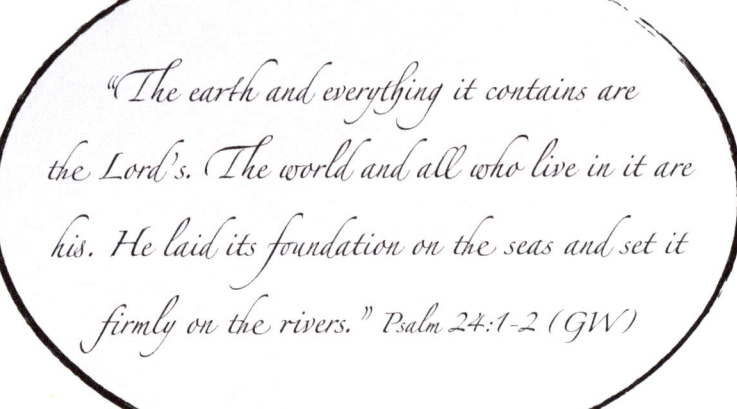

> "The earth and everything it contains are the Lord's. The world and all who live in it are his. He laid its foundation on the seas and set it firmly on the rivers." Psalm 24:1-2 (GW)

From Within

We found this masterpiece of God's creation, in an uncommon place. It was lying on the surface of macadam, like a piece of art. Unfortunately, finding it here, instead of in a nest or in a grassy area with its momma, also means that it will not be viable.

From within God makes us, shapes us.

....
....
....
....
....
....
....
....
....
....

What unexpected thing that appeared as "darkness" in your life, has He used to "birth" a change in your heart? Or to create a new dream or goal?

The Circle of Love

She has no needle and thread. She has no yarn and knitting needles. She has no loom or hands to guide her work. She is a bird, creating a cylindrical miracle, a place for her eggs, her young—a nest.

Dear Lord, may we see Your intimate love for us, in the intricacy of the bird's weaving, her nest. May we find her stitchery compelling, and as an analogy of Your lovingkindness. Help us to see how You give her instinct, insight, wisdom and creativity, that could only flow from her Creator. For in the forming of this loving circle, I see how You display, Yourself. Thank You, for holding me in the circle of Your grace. Amen.

Soul's Introspection

A nest is an amazing feat of workmanship. As birds weave a protective place for their eggs and to raise their young, a soft round sphere takes shape. From the inside, out, they fashion these masterpieces with their beaks and tiny feet. How does this marvel, show you God's provision? How does it remind you that His love encircles you? How does it display to your heart, that if He assists the birds in building a home, that He is preparing a place for you, as well?

....

....

....

....

....

....

....

....

....

....

....

....

> "There are many rooms in my Father's house, and I am going to prepare a place for you. I would not tell you this if it were not so. And after I go and prepare a place for you, I will come back and take you to myself, so that you will be where I am."
> John 14:2-3 (GNT)

> *God holds our hand when there is no one nearby, to do so.*
>
> *He collects our tears when there is no one available to dry them.*
> *(Psalm 56:8)*

....
....
....
....
....
....
....
....
....
....
....
....
....
....
....
....
....
....
....

Father God, is using every piece of your past, present and future, to show you His faithfulness. But you must do your part—make room in your heart—for Him, to be at home!

The DNA of God

Have you ever considered that God has DNA? Well, let's break down the concept of what DNA means—it is in our cells, our finger print, it's what makes us unique from one another, from a molecular perspective and through heredity. The imprint, the very hand of God, is etched upon your face. His signature, is written in the color of your eyes. His heartbeat pulses, in perfect rhythm to yours.

....
....
....
....
....
....
....
....
....
....
....
....
....

The DNA of God is upon everything and everyone that has ever been created. This is so, so that we can know and love Him, as He loves us. May our journey of discovery, lead us to magnify Him, so that we leave hereditary imprints that show our faith and devotion to our Lord. How are you amazed by this fact?

> "It's who you are and the way you live that count before God. Your worship must engage your spirit in the pursuit of truth. That's the kind of people the Father is out looking for: those who are simply and honestly themselves before him in their worship. God is sheer being itself—Spirit. Those who worship him must do it out of their very being, their spirits, their true selves, in adoration."
>
> John 4:23-24 (MSG)

The Kaleidoscope

I have been fascinated by kaleidoscopes, since I was a child. You can hold these "magical wands" up to the light, and with the tiniest twist, have an entirely different image appear before your eyes.

We are like a kaleidoscope. We have many facets. We are born into families that give our lives angles and dimensions. We have life-experiences that shape us—some are magical, some are sharp edged, but all of them magnify our character, and form the work-of-art, that we become. God shines His light upon us, then turns us, and brings our souls into focus. He magnifies certain things in our lives to transform us into His image; to create a beautiful reflection of Who He is.

So far in your journey, what has most shaped you?

*We each have flaws. We each sin and fall short.
We can dwell there, or lay these things at the feet of Jesus,
so that His love, rises, in our hearts.*

Please look up these verses, then jot a few thoughts …

Romans 3:23-24; Romans 6:23, 1 Thessalonians 3:12-13

"I have been crucified with Christ [that is, in Him I have shared His crucifixion]; it is no longer I who live, but Christ lives in me. The life I now live in the body I live by faith [by adhering to, relying on, and completely trusting] in the Son of God, who loved me and gave Himself up for me." Galatians 2:20 AMP

This verse is rich in gifts and promises. Read it a few times, then ask God to speak through each phrase.

Jesus saves us by entering the very center of our being, our hearts. Why do you think this is so? Why do you think His arms were outstretched at Calvary? Have you ever seen them as His embrace?

....
....
....
....
....
....
....
....
....
....
....
....
....
....
....

"If we confess our sins, he is faithful and just and will forgive us our sins and purify us from all unrighteousness." 1 John 1:9 NIV

Dandelion Seeds

Dandelion seeds are held in the center of this "flower" until they reach a mature stage. Then, they lift-off, to be dispersed into the air. God works on us from the inside, out—physically, emotionally and spiritually—preparing us, so that we can love and serve Him and others. We are the seeds that He uses, to produce a harvest of souls for His kingdom.

Dear Jesus, may Your image be imprinted from the inside, out—so that the seeds of Your love and influence—leave a lasting silhouette, that we belonged to You. Amen.

Seeds get planted in the soil. From below ground, they germinate and send up shoots. From the inside of darkness, they send down roots. How does this illustrate God's power to us, and that He can work within us, likewise?

....
....
....
....
....
....
....
....
....
....
....
....
....
....
....
....
....

"I will ask the Father to give you another Helper, to be with you always. He is the Spirit of truth, whom the world cannot receive, because it neither sees him nor recognizes him. But you recognize him, because he lives with you and will be in you." John 14:16-17 ISV

From the Outside Case

Have you ever felt a little like a kaleidoscope? Ordinary, plain, waiting for someone to pick you up and peer inside? To love you and show you that you're wanted and valued? Well, good news—God, your Creator, is the One Who made you originally, and loves you completely.

You may feel ordinary …
You may have been picked on as a child.
You may think you have little to offer,
But God's eye is upon you.
His love is encircling you.
His heart is reaching out to you,
To show you His love,
And your individual worth.

....
....
....
....
....
....
....
....
....
....
....
....

Man looks at the outward "case," but God is creating beauty (or handsomeness) and His image—upon the internal—the heart. It's here, that the facets of His character and love, come alive, to shine.

Doodle a verse that is special to you, displaying how God is working within your heart, to make an outward change.

"Just as water mirrors your face, so your face mirrors your heart." Proverbs 27:19 MSG

Faces, display or conceal, emotion. It's up to us, to show God's love and seek His Spirit's help, in being a light of hope. It is only through seeking the face of God, that we can do this. It is only by drawing near our Creator, that we can love every created being, as He would, and does. Does your face reflect the love of God? Do you see the Lord, in the face of others?

Smiles come from the Inside, Out

From the time that Tilly started to mature into an adult cat, we noticed that at certain angles, it appears as if she has a "painted-on" smile. It gives her the look of being perpetually happy, and feeling blessed. It is a reminder that when a smile lights our faces, we have a glow, a certain light, that comes from within.

....
....
....
....
....
....
....
....
....

"But as for me, my hope is to see Your face. When I am vindicated, I will look upon the holy face of God, and when I awake, the longing of my soul will be satisfied in the glow of Your presence." Psalm 17:15 VOICE

> "The Lord is my strength and my shield; my heart trusts in Him, and I am helped. Therefore my heart rejoices, and I praise Him with my song."
> Psalm 28:7 (HCSB)

....
....
....
....
....
....
....
....
....
....
....

Smile,
      It makes your heart feel lighter.
         Smile,
            It's like a gift you can give.
Smile,
      It's an offering of encouragement.
         Smile,
            It shows you love Jesus,
Everyday, that you live.

The Inside-Out Butterfly

The inside-out butterfly was like a moth on the outside, yet she opens to reveal brilliant blue on her interior wings. Her beauty is concealed until she rests or flies.

The longer I have photographed butterflies, the more I notice a couple of common components. 1) They must fight to come to life (from the cocoon), to fly, and they seem to have to fight for life. 2) In picture after picture, I usually notice scars, tears, marks of their journey. Sound familiar? Whether it is grays in our hair, or lines upon our face, or internal or external pain, we each bear the marks of our experiences, hurts and difficulties.

Give God every part and trust Him with the flight.

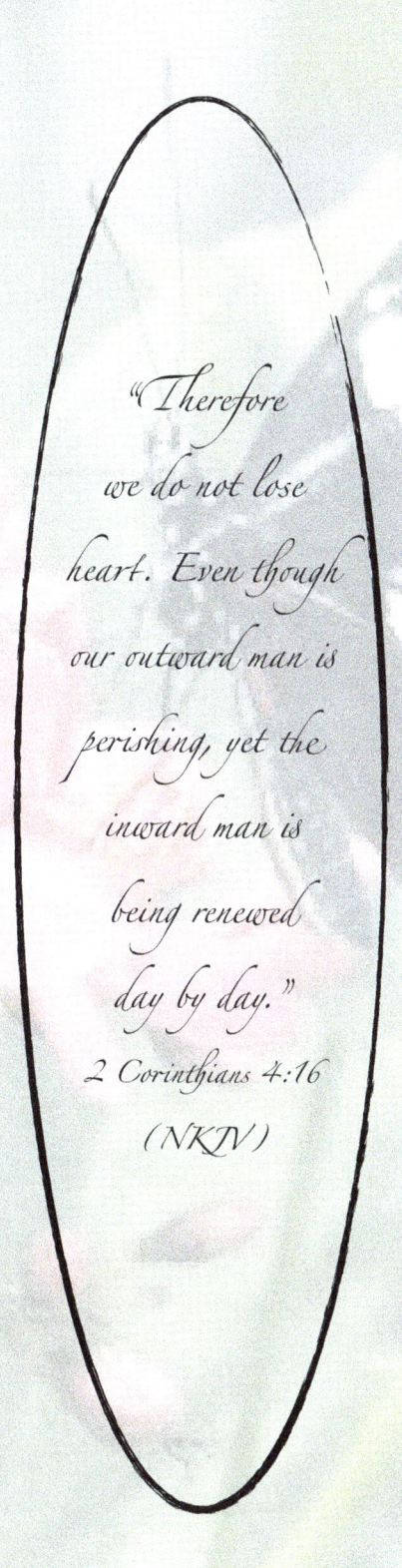

> "Therefore we do not lose heart. Even though our outward man is perishing, yet the inward man is being renewed day by day."
> 2 Corinthians 4:16 (NKJV)

Rainbow of Lights

Red, orange, yellow,
Green, blue, and lavender,
Stood silhouetted, against a wintery sky.
But the effect held a similar promise,
As the ones that God paints in the sky.
"Come into the shelter,
Of My arms, child.
Come, behold Me, on this snowy day.
Come and walk in this space of evergreens …
I am here.
I am above You.
I surround you, always.
Within the rainbow of lights,
—Know, that you are loved."

> *Have you ever felt that God was making a specific covenant or promise to your heart?*

White as Snow

Father God, I thank You, for the freshly-fallen-wonderland that was created, overnight. In the first rays of dawn, it was lovely. All that was brown and barren, was now covered as an illustration of Your grace. What looked desolate, now appeared, picturesque.

It reminds me of the verse in Isaiah 1:18 (ESV): "'Come now, let us reason together,' says the LORD. 'Though your sins are like scarlet, they will be as white as snow; though they are as red as crimson, they will become like wool.'"

*From within, we are given a covering of grace,
that is a gift to the world, outside our doors.*

We are saved by grace—not works—so that it's apparent that Immanuel lives in us. Only then, does change occur and resurrection power take over, to transform our heart and life. What is the most significant change that God has made in you?

....
....
....
....
....
....
....
....
....
....
....
....
....
....
....
....
....
....
....
....
....
....
....
....
....

Praise—From the Inside, Out

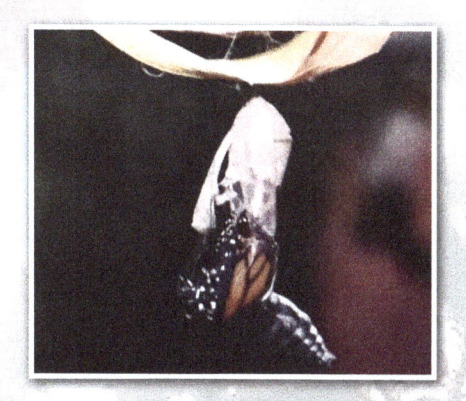

Before a butterfly can become a being of winged-beauty, it is formed and developed from the inside, out, within the confines of a cocoon. We are made similarly within the womb. Many things in life, follow this pattern such as the apple which comes from its seed, many shells hold intricate contents, and baby creatures sometimes come from eggs. What other examples come to your mind?

....

Lord, I am thankful that I am so wonderfully made.

As I ponder ....

about the workings of the human body,

I am in awe of You.

Dear Jesus, I am filled with wonder at ....

.... and

....

upon the earth and

....

....

in the heavens.

Facets of God's Love

If *love* were represented by a color—what would you choose? To some, it would be red, because it evokes the idea of romance, and expressions of the heart. To some, it might be blue, because it seems to bring a soothing, peaceful response. Perhaps you'd pick green, to remind you of Psalm 23's pasture-like scenes. Or maybe you'd choose pink or purple or orange, for their vibrancy and artistry. Or maybe Autumn's jewel-like hues, because they remind you of cool, crisp, refreshment?

No matter what shade you associate with love—whether a single primary color, a crayon-box type title, or one from the rainbow—God is reaching out, down, around—to surround your heart with His unconditional acceptance, mercy, and grace.

A kaleidoscope creates facets; so too, is God's love displayed in myriad ways—purely, joyfully, playfully, artistically—in all that He's made. What's your "love-color" and why?

....

....

....

....

....

....

....

....

....

....

....

Facets of God's Love

I loved finding the heart in the center of the tree. While you may say it was only an optical illusion—it was there—visible to those of us who paused in this moment.

God is reaching out with love to you, always. How might you be seeing it? How might you be missing it? Will you take greater notice in the future of His presence—in nature, but in your circumstances, in your day-to day routine, as well?

....
....
....
....
....
....
....
....
....
....
....
....
....
....
....
....
....
....
....
....
....

The facets of God's love, surround us in all of nature. From the sea, to the sky, to the trees, to the birdsong—everything that He has made—is a lyric, a line-by-line detailing of His care for all humanity. May it touch your heart today, for the first time, or with a fresh passion, that inspires your appreciation and praise.

"And I am convinced that nothing can ever separate us from God's love."
Romans 8:38a NLT

*He is
the Vine,
we are
the branches;
attached to Him
we bear
fruit.
Alone,
we can do
nothing.*

Up in the Tree Tops

I was looking out my little kitchen window one morning when we lived in Hawaii, to have the thought that …"up above the tree tops, lives our Father." Yet, as high as the heavens are above us, if we have accepted Jesus as the Lord of our lives, then He lives within our hearts, too. I loved this idea. And as I look at God's wondrous creations, I find myself in awe of the, Creator. Though He is invisible, He is visible, through all that His hands have made.

Up in the tree tops, high above … lives the God of love. But if you call Him Lord, He lives within you, too. And if you ask Him, He will help you become more aware of His beauty. He will make all that is invisible, visible to your soul. Because when we truly grasp that He is in us, we might just see a whole lot of things—through the light of His love. What has you "looking up," today?

Soul's Introspection

Love is solid, it's fluid. It's an emotion. It's a noun. It's a verb.

What has the Lord entrusted to you, that He wants you to share? Your home? Your resources? Your talents? Your testimony? Your prayer-warrior spirit? Your family? Your heart with a child, a widow/widower? Your time to volunteer?

"The Lord is compassionate and gracious, patient, and abundantly rich in gracious love."
Psalm 103:8 ISV

Love is the Scroll

The earth and heavens are His scroll, unfurled for the human heart. But will you believe? Will you receive all that He longs to communicate to your heart? For it is love, true love, that is displayed, everyday!

Love is the Scroll,
To be unrolled ...
Will you read it,
With your heart?
For it is the very heart of God,
Written for you.

"... Pay attention to my words—incline your ear to my sayings. Do not let them out of your sight, keep them within your heart. For they are life to those who find them and health to their whole body. Guard your heart diligently, for from it flow the springs of life."
Proverbs 4:20-23 TLV

....

....

....

....

....

....

....

....

....

....

....

....

....

....

....

....

The Bible tells to "do unto others as we would have them do unto us," to "be kind, tender-hearted, forgiving" to "bless those who curse us." Do you find these instructions to be difficult at times? What encourages you to obey God's decrees? How can we find creative ways to witness to the lost? How do we persevere in loving others—in our workplace, in lines, etc. and teach our kids, grandkids, and those we influence, to do likewise? How can we be an example of these virtues in our modern world?

Encircling Love

There was rose, pearl,
Lavender, gold and blue;
These surrounded,
A silver storybook moon,
It's true.

And I saw Your love, God,
Everlasting,
Never-ending,
Unfathomable—
Reaching out.
It encircles every nation,
Embraces all of mankind.

The encircling love of Jesus was displayed so beautifully, on this morning. It is available to every heart, always. Has His light, touched your soul?

Showers as a Blessing

Dear Lord,
I will see the rain as a shower of blessing. I will see Your watering of the earth, as a sign of Your care and provision for my every need.

I will feel Your Spirit, like a waterfall of goodness— cleansing, restoring and filling me with Your strength, joy and love.

In every circumstance and happening in my life, I feel drenched with Your grace.

The rain reminds me, that You reign over all of earth and heaven.

I trust You Father, because many times, rain, is followed by a rainbow. And I know that no matter what happens, You hold every day of my life, in Your hands.
Amen.

"God stretched out the northern sky and hung the earth in empty space. It is God who fills the clouds with water and keeps them from bursting with the weight. He hides the full moon behind a cloud. He divided light from darkness by a circle drawn on the face of the sea."
Job 26:7-10 GNT

Drenched

In my photo,
The Rose of Sharon,
Is drenched.

The rain has come,
And saturated its petals.
The leaves and stems,
Every part of the flower,
Has been covered in heaven's dew.

I wondered if we are drenched,
In His love,
In His mercy,
In His grace,
In His power?

"Drip down, O heavens, from above, and let the clouds pour down righteousness; let the earth open up and salvation bear fruit, and righteousness spring up with it. I, the Lord, have created it." Isaiah 45:8 NASB

Are we living under the reign, of His submission? Do we allow Jesus to saturate our minds, our moods, our emotions, with His thoughts and ways? Are we seeking His strength, and listening for His voice? Do we allow Him to enfold us, in our everyday decisions?

Jesus gave His life for us, in order to show His love for all mankind. John 3:16-17 (GW), confirms this truth. Below are these verses. Where it says "the world," if you have never done so, insert your name. "God loved the world (your name here) this way: He gave his only Son so that everyone (you) who believes in Him will not die but will have eternal life. God sent his Son into the world, not to condemn the world, but to save the world." This is His personal invitation to your heart.

How does this exercise, give you a fresh insight into Jesus' life and death and resurrection? How does it help you appreciate that He became your ransom?

....
....
....
....
....
....
....
....
....
....
....
....
....
....

"Beloved, let us love one another, for love is of God; and everyone who loves is born of God and knows God." 1 John 4:7 NKJV

Prisms Shining

When we lived in Virginia, I would decorate the bureau that sat in our entry way, with seasonal designs. Often, I would enhance my creative floral creations with light, such as the prism-inducing one, that is present. We have a few that we rotated for the applicable themes.

We came to the time of our moving, and learned that we were not the only ones to enjoy their illumination. Unbeknownst to us, our prisms were visible to the neighbors.

Prisms shone from our home to bring peace to the hearts of others. That's what a relationship with Jesus does, in the heart, mind and soul, of His child. Is your light shining, in your world?

Crown of Life

Since the kids in our neighborhood were being home-schooled due to the Corona Virus, we were treated to many displays of their artistry. Our sidewalks, rocks, and even windows, contained any number of drawings and appliqués to display their imaginations—come to life.

This, happens to be one of my favorite designs. There was something about a rainbow wreath (or crown) made of hearts, that I loved.

....
....
....
....
....
....
....
....
....
....
....
....
....

The love of God is like a circle, because it creates in us a sense of completion, while at the same time, makes everyone (who calls upon the name of the Lord), welcome. There is always room to be included in the crown of His family. There is no heart that is or will be excluded, from the coming design that shall be formed of those who worship around His throne. For those who love Jesus, He loves forever. And this love knows no end. May He be praised. And may each of us be found around the throne, to crown Him, Lord of All. Describe a few ways that God's love encircles you.

"Do not let kindness and truth leave you; bind them around your neck, write them on the tablet of your heart. So you will find favor and good repute in the sight of God and man." Proverbs 3:3-4 NASB

....
....
....
....
....
....
....
....
....
....
....
....
....
....
....
....
....
....
....
....
....

We can convey love in many ways. For instance: we give gifts, we give of ourselves, we make things, (bake things) to show we care, we serve, we offer compliments or send notes of encouragement. How do you respond to love? How do you offer it? What makes you, and those around you, feel loved? Does your environment affect your emotional response?

The Connection of Love

We were attending an outdoor church service, when I observed this scene: a little tike began to draw on the pavement. But what caught my attention? Each of his little vignettes—were joined with a connecting line. He drew each vehicle separately, but then created of them, one picture. I found this, intriguing.

After the service I chatted with his mom. She told us his name, that he was 3 1/2, and that I was correct in my spying out of his art—as many forms of transportation. She said that he has all of these as toys, and that they are currently his favorite things.

Everything that God has made, is likewise, individual. Whether it is a sunrise, a flower, a new baby, a stalk of grain ... in His hands, creation as a whole, represents Who He is to us, every day. We decide how much we notice, how much we observe ... but never doubt that each object or landscape or grouping, is meant to draw us, near Him.

List a few things that you are noticing today, in column 1. And list how they are connected (or what they have in common), in column 2.

....	....
....	....
....	....
....	....
....	....
....	....
....	....
....	....
....	....
....	....

Jeremiah 31:3 tells us, that the Lord "has drawn us with loving-kindness." To me, this means two things.
1) He created us—drew us, sketched us, made us—with love.
2) He draws us—invites us, comforts us, pulls us into sweet friendship and fellowship. How does this verse make you feel?

Does this double meaning bring a fresh perspective of these words?

....

....

....

....

....

....

....

....

....

....

....

....

....

....

....

....

....

....

....

....

....

....

....

....

Let your child, grandchild, or a young friend create a small drawing in the space below. Give thanks for them in your life. What insight can you glean from the inspiration that they created?

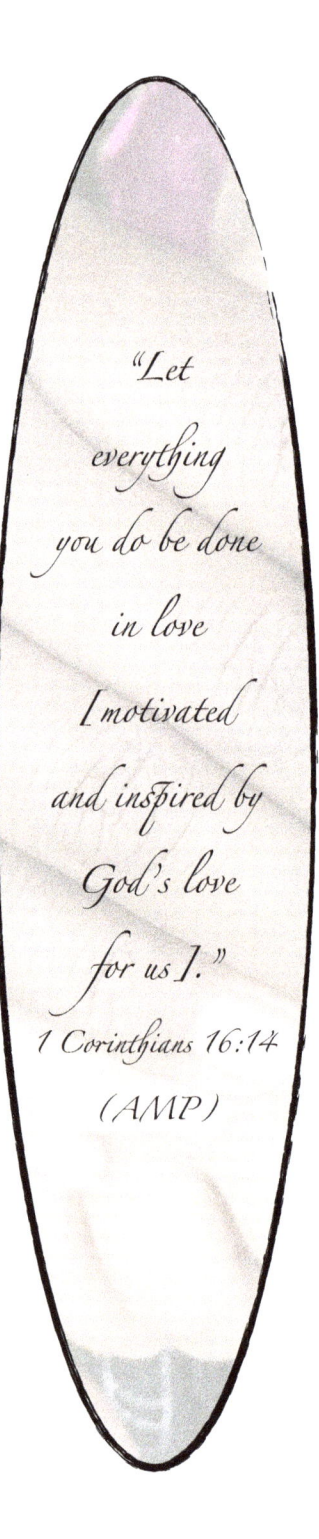

"Let everything you do be done in love [motivated and inspired by God's love for us]."
1 Corinthians 16:14 (AMP)

The Heart of Prayer

If you draw a heart in the air,
As a child would do,
You will see in the end,
That it returns to you.
But not until,
It rises upward;
Not until,
It goes outward.
And to me,
This is a way,
To shape our prayers.
It is a reminder,
To lift our praises,
Every care,
And to cover,
One another's,
Needs.

The heart that prays, extends love by lifting others up. We are reaching outward, connecting one another with God's grace. And as we touch those we care about, our focus is turned on the One Who loves us, unconditionally.

Prayer, is like sending our innermost thoughts through the tube of a kaleidoscope, directly to the heart of God. Then His Spirit takes them, and gives them facets, interceding on our behalf to turn them into prisms, that shine as we cover our family, friends, strangers, our nation. What rainbows must be created, as He turns our whispers into treasures of love.

....
....
....
....
....
....
....
....
....
....
....

Every Hue

Each shade of the rocks was brought out, by the tide.

Their colors were made vibrant, by the cleansing, God supplied.

Every soul upon the earth, is loved and cherished, given worth.

Renewed, restored, by His cleansing flood, when we receive, the gift of His grace-filled blood.

I think God made every hue in creation, to reflect to our hearts, that every one will be represented around His throne.

What glory shall shine from every countenance, as we lay down our crowns to worship and adore Jesus, our Lord!

Are you held in the arms of the Rock, so that He is bringing out every hue of His grace in your life?

What's on your heart? Jesus longs to hear your request, concerns, or praise.

....
....
....
....
....
....
....
....
....
....
....
....
....
....
....
....
....
....

Prayer, joins our hands and our hearts — across a table, across miles, and across the world — with the gift of love.

Prayer changes things!

Creation, Whispered and Shouted

God has made wondrous, bold, beautiful, stunning and creative things for us to see and enjoy. They are like a shout of His might, glory and power. Then He's made the unique, the fragrant, the intoxicating, to draw us in, closer, to whisper of His sovereignty, grace, joy, peace, and hope. And if we were to observe and understand all of creation—God's intention would be to show us His nature—the very essence of His love and faithfulness.

....
....
....
....
....
....

Creation, has been whispered and shouted, so that everyone can see something of God's grandeur and holiness. Through it, His nature is clearly on display. And by it, His character and attributes have been made known. Are you listening? Are you observant?

"For You, Lord, are kind and ready to forgive, rich in faithful love to all who call on You." Psalm 86:5 HCSB

....

....

....

....

....

....

....

....

....

....

....

....

....

....

....

....

God's forgiveness, is described in Psalm 103:12, as reaching "as far as the East is from the West." How does this promise, make you feel, loved? How does it affirm His affection and acceptance of your heart? How does it draw you toward your Maker and Creator?

Golden Light of His Love

> Through the trees,
> Swept the light.
>> It faded past the shadows,
>> To the meadow, below.
>>> My eyes raised upward,
>>> To the Light, above.
>>>> It was like beholding,
>>>> God's golden rays of love.

Your Light, Oh Lord, is all around us. Just like the sun, Your love touches every surface, every thing in heaven and earth. You make all of creation glow with Your radiance. And when Your hope sweeps o're a soul, it is lit from within, to draw others to You.

God's love, is the light that flows from heaven—into our hearts and onto all of creation.

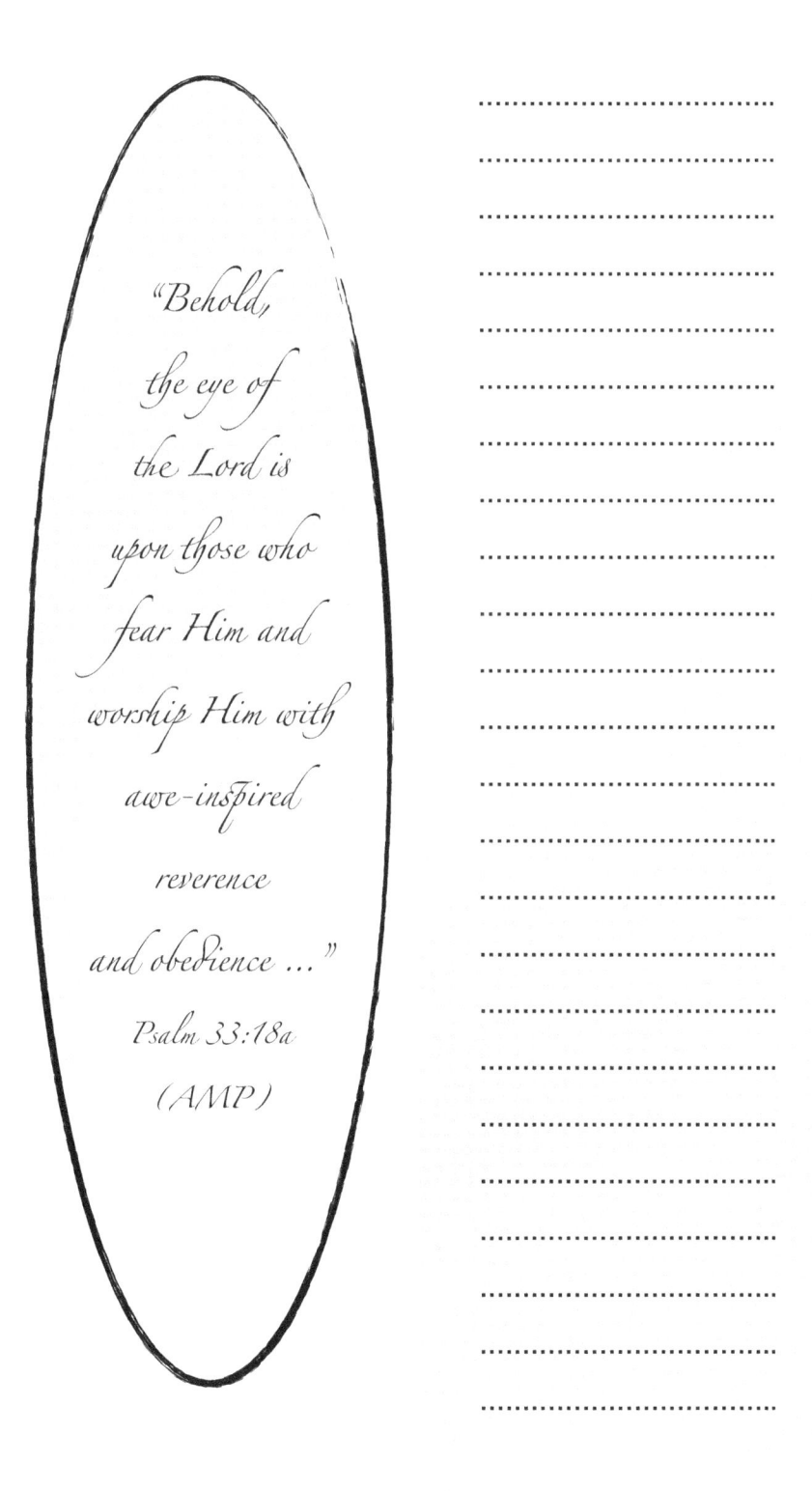

> "Behold, the eye of the Lord is upon those who fear Him and worship Him with awe-inspired reverence and obedience …"
> Psalm 33:18a (AMP)

Nourishing

Rain, falls, to nourish the earth. It makes all things grow. It is God's love poured out upon the land in order to make flowers, plants and crops, flourish. Snow, falls in its season to continue the cycle, to form sculptures—snowflakes, drifts, icicles—shapes, that are held until the temperatures rise.

Love is liquid, fluid. Love is moving, enriching; It's a life-giving nutrient.

....

....

....

....

....

....

....

Love flowed from the veins of Jesus, into the hearts of all mankind. How is God's love nourishing you?

Love is a living thing; it's a flowing thing. It's a nourishing, cleansing, restoring, renewing thing. It is needed for us to survive. And Jesus' love was perfect. It is available in every season. And it is His desire that we love Him as He loves us. It's His desire that we love others, likewise.

....
....
....
....
....
....
....
....
....
....
....
....
....
....
....
....
....
....
....
....
....
....
....
....
....
....
....
....
....
....
....
....

May God's love that ran so richly through His veins, flow into ours, so that we are like rain and snow, nourishing everyone that we encounter with seeds of faith.

1 Corinthians 13:7 (NLT) says this: "Love never gives up, never loses faith, is always hopeful, and endures through every circumstance." Do you find these words easy or hard to live out? Now think of them as a promise from Jesus. He never gives us, never loses faith, is always hopeful and endures forever. How does this promise feel, now? How do we love this way, in our uncertain world?

....

....

....

....

....

....

....

....

....

....

....

....

....

....

....

....

"I pray that from his glorious, unlimited resources he will empower you with inner strength through his Spirit. Then Christ will make his home in your hearts as you trust in him. Your roots will grow down into God's love and keep you strong. And may you have the power to understand, as all God's people should, how wide, how long, how high, and how deep his love is." Ephesians 3:16-18 NLT

One Heart of Love

We are given …

2 Eyes …
2 Ears …
2 Hands …
2 Feet …

But only 1 Heart …

So it must be,
Big enough …

To Love …
To Give …
To Share …
To Reflect, Jesus.

....
....
....
....
....
....
....
....
....
....
....
....
....

How will you use your 1 heart, 2 eyes, 2 ears,
2 hands and feet, to love God and others?

"But God demonstrates His own love toward us, in that while we were still sinners, Christ died for us." Romans 5:8 NKJV

What simple or extravagant act of kindness have you given someone? What is the sweetest gift that you have ever received? Who gave it to you? How did you respond?

Gazing with Wonder

Our eyes, hold our emotions; they give us not only vision to see the world, but also allow the world to see something of our feelings—joy, light, love, sorrow, pain—is reflected, highlighted, mirrored. These tiny windows, help us glimpse not only the wonder of God's creation, the beauty in each other, but also allow each of us to see some of His grandeur in every thing that He has ever made.

Dear Jesus, let each of us—feel to the depths of our soul—that we are the apple of Your eye. May Your love, Your grace, Your hope and truth, permeate our emotions, our thoughts, and circumstances, until we can feel Your embrace of kindness, goodness, and tenderness, like a physical touch. Thank You, for watching over us. Thank You, for your observant notice and care. Help us, fix our eyes upon You. Amen.

> "The Lord keeps watch over you as you come and go, both now and forever."
> Psalm 121:8 (NLT)

Eyes only for You

Our eyes are like a camera lens; in less than a second, we can go from seeing a landscape, to focusing in on the minutest detail. Our eyes are sharper and faster at this transition, than a mechanical device. Our Creator—created us with these built-in-miracles, to absorb, to observe—not only His creations, but to see the very hand and presence of God, in bursts, that are faster than the speed of light.

- But do we notice the beauty right before us?
- Do we see Your glory God?
- Do we see the landscape, the fullness of Your grace that is constantly unfolding?
- Do we observe the detail, the colors, the nuances—of sky, earth, birds, flowers—of every human face?
- Do we focus on what a miracle it is, to be given physical and spiritual vision?

If our eyes are focused on the Creator, we are captivated by His nature, everyday, every moment, until we see Him face to face. In what ways, do you give Him honor and glory?

....
....
....
....
....
....
....
....
....
....
....
....
....
....
....

Look up,
Look into,
The eyes of grace.
Let them hold you,
In the gaze,
Of purest love.

Immeasurable

God's love is as measureless,
As the ocean's width, breadth and depth.

    It reaches as far,
    As the East is from the West.

        It's as enduring as He is,
        From beginning to end,
        And from everlasting to everlasting.

            God's love reaches out to us, (mankind),
            No matter where we live,
            Work or play.

                It is invisible,
                Yet visibly,
                Felt, seen, and experienced.

....

....

....

....

....

Immeasurable, is the love of God, so that it cannot be missed or contained or tamed. And it is available to one and all. He loved us perfectly at our birth. He loves and redeems us, at our re-birth. He loves us always, eternally. Oh, what a gift to the soul!

....
....
....
....
....
....
....
....
....
....
....
....
....

Have you been re-born?

God's love
transcends
all time and space.

He demonstrated
it at Calvary where
He physically took
our place.

But His love
indwells the heart
and soul—
internally,
eternally—that is
surrendered.

His Spirit teaches
us to live,
sacrificially,
according to His
Will, and by
faith.

This love, has
been a witness
and a testimony
that has been
passed down
through every
generation, from
the time that Jesus
was born as a
babe.

And He died and
rose from the
grave, to rule and
reign, always.

If you had an absent dad, a distant father, or one who often traveled for his work—you may have a skewed view of Jesus' love. It's sometimes hard for these individuals to grasp how wide and high and deep God's love—reaches, stretches, moves.

You cannot outrun it. You cannot do anything to prevent it. You cannot outlast it. You cannot outmaneuver it. You cannot hide from it. So how about trying to surrender!

Ask Jesus to teach you that His love has no limits, and you may be surprised how little by little (or in great strides) you learn to trust Him. Try it!

If you feel His nudge, give in! Stop striving to do life on your own, give Him control. Rest. Come under His pinions. God loves you—strongly, purely, eternally. Run, don't walk. Come home. Get yourself loved, today! What is God's Spirit speaking to your soul? See Romans 3:23-34, 6:23, 10:9-10, and Ephesians 2:8-9 for inspiration.

> "Your life must be controlled by love, just as Christ loved us and gave his life for us as a sweet-smelling offering and sacrifice that pleases God."
> Ephesian 5:2 (GNT)

The Shades of God's Love

In the shades of Your love,
I walk, I dance.
By the light of Your Spirit,
I'm touched by Salvation's romance.
        In the shadow of Your love,
        I take hold of Your hand,
        Moving within the living rainbow reflected here,
        At the edge of the sand.
                Until, until …
                Eternity meets me today,
                Until the moment,
                That I behold Your holy face.

The Lord shades us in His love, to keep us stepping and dancing, in the close company of God.

....
....
....
....
....
....
....
....
....
....
....
....
....
....
....
....
....
....
....
....

"He saved us because of his mercy and not because of any good things that we have done. God washed us by the power of the Holy Spirit. He gave us new birth and a fresh beginning. God sent Jesus Christ our Savior to give us his Spirit. Jesus treated us much better than we deserve. He made us acceptable to God and gave us the hope of eternal life." Titus 3:5-7 CEV

> "Love is patient and kind. Love is not jealous or boastful or proud or rude. It does not demand its own way. It is not irritable, and it keeps no record of being wronged. It does not rejoice about injustice but rejoices whenever the truth wins out. Love never gives up, never loses faith, is always hopeful, and endures through every circumstance."
> 1 Corinthians 13:4-7 NLT

Most of us have heard these verses as part of a wedding or sermon. Right? Well, one day in my personal devotional time, the Lord reversed them. What do I mean?

He spoke them into my heart as double negatives. For instance—love is not impatient. Love is not unkind. Love does not (verses 4 and 7)... I found it interesting and impactful to hear them this way. And while this may not be proper grammar, it provided another lesson in what love is, and is not.

How might this little exercise assist you, in seeing God's intention of the love chapter? How might it clarify how we are to live and emulate His life?

If you have breath in your lungs, God is not finished with your life, with your mission. This means that He loves you, believes in you, and means for you to do something with this moment and every one that you have to enjoy. How does this convey His love for you? How does it convey His unconditional promise to your soul? Does it make you want to change anything in your life? Reprioritize anything? Or cause you to make any fresh commitments in your "following?"

....
....
....
....
....
....
....
....
....
....
....
....
....
....
....
....
....

"Not to us, O Lord, not to us, but to your name goes all the glory for your unfailing love and faithfulness." Psalm 115:1 NLT

> If you viewed your life as miracle, what would you do, for the cause of Christ?
>
> *"How blessed is God! And what a blessing he is! He's the Father of our Master, Jesus Christ, and takes us to the high places of blessing in him. Long before he laid down earth's foundations, he had us in mind, had settled on us as the focus of his love, to be made whole and holy by his love. Long, long ago he decided to adopt us into his family through Jesus Christ. (What pleasure he took in planning this!) He wanted us to enter into the celebration of his lavish gift-giving by the hand of his beloved Son."* Ephesians 1:3-6 (MSG)

....
....
....
....
....
....
....
....
....
....
....
....
....
....
....

"This is the embodiment of true love: not that we have loved God first, but that He loved us and sent His unique Son on a special mission to become an atoning sacrifice for our sins."
1 John 4:10 VOICE

Have you ever written a love letter to Jesus?
Now is your opportunity:

....

....

....

....

....

....

....

....

....

....

> *"Kindness, peace, love—may they never stop blooming in you and from you."* Jude 1:2 (VOICE)

Praise—Facets of God's Love

Heart designs are often synonymous with the communication of love. And I appreciate finding them in nature. To me, ones like my Ginkgo leaves below, are constant reminders of God's unending, fathomless love for us, in every season.

In the spaces below, list some of the things you love,

....

some of the people you love and those who love you,

....

a few reasons that you appreciate God's unconditional love.

....

What is the sweetest act of love that you have received?

....

What is the sweetest act of love that you have given?

....

With which sense do you most keenly feel or experience love?

....

May the words we say, and the meditation of our heart,
be the offering of love and praise unto Your ear, O God.

It's our prayer that you've been encouraged by
Volume 1 of the Creation's Kaleidoscope: Embracing Light *Journal.*

Blessings! *deborah goshorn-stenger*
2 Pause and Praise Creations

Dear Reader,

Will you leave a kind or thoughtful review?

Now that you've finished using this journal, will you tell us what you think? Did this guided-style of journal, encourage you to meet with God, daily? How has it spoken to your heart? How has it helped you to grow in your relationship with Jesus, or given you a greater awareness of Jesus' love, through creation?

We'd be honored if you take time to leave us a comment (wherever you've purchased our product, i.e. Amazon, etc.). Please also include your previous journaling experience on a 0 to 5 scale. 0 being none, and 5 being experienced. We'll use your feedback to guide any updates to this manuscript, as well as consider your inputs for future projects.

Would you like to be added to our mailing list?

Do you want to be notified of upcoming releases and exclusive materials? If so, we invite you to join our mailing list.

You can do so, at our website:

2pauseandpraisecreations.com

Thank you so much!
Doug and Deb